City Girl,
Country Girl

City Girl,
Country Girl

Marian Brandes Gilligan

To order additional copies of this book, contact:
Xlibris Corporation
1-888-795-4274
www.Xlibris.com
Orders@Xlibris.com

36103

CONTENTS

I dedicate this story to my husband, Tom, our children—Tom, Bob, Kathy, Kim, and Jeff, and their spouses—and our grandchildren.

PROLOGUE

I have written this story of my life in the hope that the younger generations will realize there are struggles in all of our lives.

The tragic circumstances of my early life gave me a deep faith in God and complete comfort in my religion. In each loss of a loved one I found many wonderful people who were always there to help.

It is my wish that you will come away from this story with a strong sense of the need to persevere, to work hard to support yourself and not expect that it is anyone's responsibility but your own, and to live a good, purposeful life. And to have faith that God will help you through difficult times.

Stand up for what is right, even if you stand alone.

Marian Brandes Gilligan
November 1, 2006

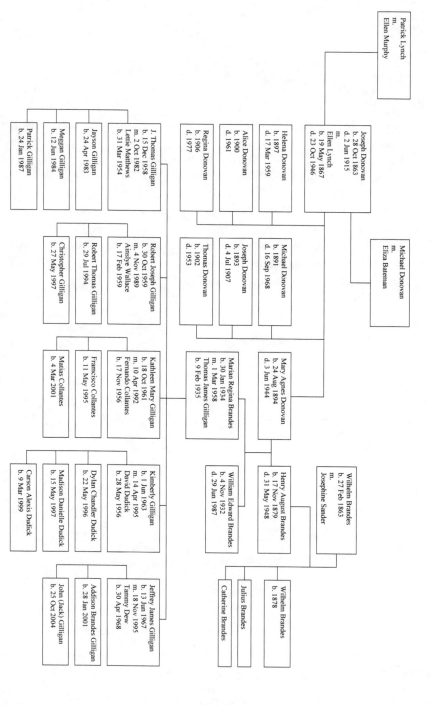

Family Tree

THIS IS THE STORY OF MY JOURNEY THROUGH LIFE AND THE KINDNESS OF OTHERS TOWARDS ME

My parents were immigrants, making me a first generation American. While I'm proud of my Irish and German heritage, I'm even more proud of being American, especially since America provided my family with opportunities and freedom.

When my parents left their respective homelands—with no way of anticipating the blessings and sorrows they would face—they knew in their hearts they might never again see the loved ones they left behind. The long, difficult trip across the Atlantic took approximately one week, during which many passengers, including children, lost their lives. I am so impressed with how brave these people were to travel to a new country to try to create better lives for themselves and their families.

My mother's family in Ireland

My maternal grandfather (born around 1867, and surnamed O'Donovan, which was shortened upon arrival in the U.S. to Donovan) was originally a police constable in County Cork. When he married the woman who would become my grandmother—Ellen Lynch (also born about 1867), a teacher from Dingle, County Kerry—he became a shopkeeper on Dingle's Main Street. The entire family lived over the shop, which still stands today.

Grandfather Donovan was sponsored by relatives in Pittsburgh, PA, and was the first to come to the U.S., in either 1896 or 1897. After he took a job in a steel mill, he sent for my grandmother and their four children, the third of which, Mary Agnes, would become my mother. Mother had been baptized in St Mary's Catholic Church in Dingle, and was three years old when she came to America. They traveled aboard the Campania from Queenstown, Ireland to Ellis Island, New York. They later took a train to Pittsburgh, Pennsylvania where they settled at 1119 Liberty Street.

Some of my grandmother's cousins still live in a picturesque hamlet on the family farm outside of Dingle, in a village called Ballenasig. Great-grandmother Murphy-Lynch and grandmother Lynch-Donovan were both born there.

Several years ago, Tom and I visited Ireland and met my cousin, Paddy Lynch—a sheep farmer—and his family. He and his wife, Mariead, are wonderful people, very down-to-earth and easy to know. Paddy's father was my mother's first cousin. His grandfather and my grandmother were sister and brother. When we visited the still fertile family farm, Paddy gave us the opportunity to visit the old house, right next door, where my grandmother grew up.

The first floor of what I lovingly call our ancestral home had two rooms, both with dirt floors. One room was used as a shelter by the farm animals brought in on cold winter nights; the other was a combination kitchen and living room. Cooking was done in the fireplace that filled the room. There was no electricity, running water, or indoor plumbing.

A ladder was built into the wall of this room, and Tom and I climbed up to see the loft where my great-grandparents and their seven children slept. The last people to live in this house were Paddy's parents and siblings. Their lifestyle was so different from what we're used to. The house opposite this one is where my great-grandmother grew up, but it's now used for storage and we didn't go in.

My mother's family in the States

After a few years working in the steel mill, my grandfather decided to open a grocery store in the small town of Homestead, just outside of Pittsburgh. By now, he and grandmother had three American-born children to go along with the four who were born in Ireland. Life was improving, but bad luck soon crossed the family's path.

My mother's brother—Uncle Josie—was nearing his 14th birthday when he and a group of friends were playing in the local park with the service revolver Grandfather had brought from Ireland. The gun accidentally fired, fatally wounding Uncle Josie. Grandfather rushed to the park and carried Josie home, where he died on the porch in Grandmother's arms.

A few years later, Grandfather died of pneumonia. Grandmother tried to sell the business but so many customers had put their groceries on the "tab" (in other words, hadn't paid their bills); there was no money to be made. Income was so tight that my grandmother cleaned houses and took in laundry to make ends meet.

Mother's oldest brother, Mike, went to work in a steel mill and the other children who were old enough helped by doing chores and odd jobs. They saved every possible cent because Uncle Mike decided it would be wonderful to go into farming again, just as his grandparents had done in Ireland. When he eventually saw a newspaper advertisement for a farm outside of Newburgh, NY, adjacent to the Hudson River, Uncle Mike decided to act.

He took the train from Pittsburgh to New York City, and then transferred to another train to reach Newburgh. As soon as he saw the farm—98 acres of workable land—he knew it was what he wanted. Before returning to Homestead, he signed papers for the property.

Uncle Mike gathered my grandmother, his sister Regina, brother Tom, and all their belongings, put them into a horse and carriage, and drove to Newburgh. The farm quickly became a second home for all of the Donovans. During vacations, my mother and aunts would visit and help with the farm work. I always had a fondness for the farm and, eventually, it became home for me, too.

MY FATHER'S FAMILY IN GERMANY AND ITALY

Although I was very close with my father—Henry August Brandes—I know very little of his younger life, other than that he came from Braunschweig, Germany, and that his last name was quite common there (much as Smith and Jones are in the States). He was the only one of his siblings—brothers Wilhelm and Julius, and sister Catherine—to come to America.

Father spoke about Wilhelm quite often, and my brother was named after him. Father faithfully stayed in touch with his family until World War II when all correspondence between Germany, Italy, and the United States was disrupted. He never heard from his family again, and assumed they were all killed during the allied bombings.

After my paternal grandparents were married, Grandfather Brandes was chosen to run the family business in Naples. (They owned a gilding business in Braunschweig, but also had branches in Naples and Milan.) They brought a German cook with them and, when the children were old enough to learn, they had a German tutor come to Italy to teach them academics.

Shortly after the death of his mother, my father—at the age of 24—left Naples for the U.S. (This was discovered by our daughter, Kathy.) I believe Grandfather Brandes had remarried by the time my father left for America. My father left Naples, Italy aboard the SS Lahn to Ellis Island, New York.

LIFE IN THE
UNITED STATES

When my father came to the States he took a job teaching languages at a local high school while going through an American physician recertification process. He spoke seven languages, including English.

Both of my parents were in the medical field, my mother a registered nurse and my father a doctor (a general practitioner). Although I don't know for sure, I believe my parents met through their mutual profession.

I was born on January 30, 1934 in the New York Medical Center in New York City. I was brought home to an apartment house at 2255 Bedford Avenue in the Flatbush section of Brooklyn. My brother, William, fifteen months older than me, was no longer an only child.

We lived a pretty normal life. My brother and I had problems with asthma and allergies, but our parents' knowledge of medicine and patient care must have been a big help with our health problems.

Two of my mother's sisters lived in Brooklyn. Helen (Helena), who lived about four blocks from us, was a Western Union Telegraph operator. Alice, who lived about 30 minutes away by subway in the Greenpoint section of Brooklyn, was a registered nurse at Greenpoint Eye and Ear Hospital.

Mother's youngest sister, Regina, worked as a secretary at DuPont's Newburgh facility where she met her future husband, Bill Anderson, a chemist whose family lived in Newburgh.

My mother, the third oldest, had two older brothers, Mike and Josie. She also had a brother, Tom, who was the second youngest child. Mike and Tom lived with Grandmother Donovan on the farm in New Windsor, outside of Newburgh, NY. Only three of my grandparents' six remaining children were married: my mother, Aunt Helena and Aunt Regina.

Mother was the tallest of the four girls, about 5'5", with a medium build. She had dark brown hair (almost black) which she combed straight back and fastened into a bun in the back of her head. Her eyes were hazel, as were all the Donovan girls'. (The brothers all had blue eyes.) Her complexion was fair, and I remember her always wearing a housedress, which was not unusual back then.

Dad was only a few inches taller than Mother, perhaps 5'7" (although his immigration papers list him as 5'8"). He had a medium to husky build, snow-white hair, olive complexion—similar to mine—and dark brown eyes.

Aunt Helena would often visit our apartment on Bedford Avenue and talk with Mother about moving into a house where we could all live together. Aunt Helena's husband had no interest in working, so she left him and raised her son, Tommy Fagan, by herself. Whenever Aunt Helen visited, mother always fixed a pot of tea, a tradition that continued after we moved to Woods Place, just a block-and-a-half away.

Mother used loose leaves to brew tea, and both she and Aunt Helena always got some in their cups. Their ritual included adding milk to their tea and having a little sweet goodie with it. They would always drain their cups, leaving the tea leaves for Aunt Helena to read. My aunt had a delightful personality, was superstitious (as were many Irish, including Mother) and the stories she concocted from reading the leaves were a riot. To know Aunt Helena was to love her. She was a quite a lady.

OUR FIRST HOUSE

When I was five years old, I started kindergarten in the Brooklyn public school system. And about a year later—in 1940—mother and Aunt Helena had their wish come true: we all moved to a private home at 22 Woods Place. There were only three houses on our side of the street, plus a large, enclosed auto repair business. This brick garage structure was bigger than all three houses put together, but it was very neat and there were never any cars parked outside.

Directly across the street from us were about fifteen single car garages that people rented to house their cars. Each garage was very small compared to what we're used to today, but the cars of that era were smaller, too. Even with all the autos, our street was very quiet because cars were used mostly on weekends or for trips, and virtually everyone used public transportation—trolleys and subways—during the week.

The fare back in the '40s was only a nickel. Today, of course, it's around two dollars. In the 1950s, buses replaced trolleys, although it took many years until the trolley tracks were finally removed. The subway trains still exist.

Our house at Woods Place was great: big enough for all of us. Aunt Helena and her son, Tommy, who was about ten years older than me, lived on the top floor. When World War II broke out, Tommy joined the Navy. (I don't think he ever graduated from high school.) My family lived on the main floor, with a living room in the front, bedrooms in the back and a large kitchen in the basement.

The kitchen had a potbelly stove that heated the room. Behind the kitchen was a furnace room with two coal bins that supplied heat for the radiators upstairs and a storage area. It was common back then for a house to have only one bathroom and ours was no different. Even though the one bathroom was on the top floor, we were so happy with our house we really didn't mind.

Although we lived in the city, it didn't seem like it. There were large old maple trees in both the front and back yard between our house and the house next door. Lots of bushes and morning glories grew on the front fence. In the back yard, Mother planted fruit trees, and she had a vegetable garden and a grape arbor for making jelly.

We rented the house from the people who lived next door at 24 Woods Place. It had originally been owned by Thomas Bennett, who had been married to a woman named Bridget Mason. (Both had passed away years before we rented it.) Bridgett's unmarried younger sisters, Mary and Annie Mason—both in their 70s—now lived in the house, along with two people in their 40s who had been raised by the Bennetts; Julia (Sis) Pigott and Walter (Brother) Rooney.

Annie's real name was Margaret Ann, but everyone called her Annie. In her younger days, she had been a cook for a wealthy Brooklyn family by the name of Ditmas, and Mary had worked as a housekeeper at a rectory. Brother Rooney, who was very handy and took care of the maintenance of both homes, and Sis Pigott both had good jobs and assisted the Masons sisters.

When we moved into our little house none of us knew the impact we would have on the people we rented from and they on our lives.

The one-family house at the end of our street was owned by Mrs. Henry, who lived there with her grandson, Lawrence. Her upper floor was used as a rental, and when we lived on the block, the O'Loughlin's and their four children lived there. The oldest was about five or six years younger than me. My brother sometimes played with Lawrence Henry, who was about a year older than he was.

When we first moved to Woods Place, my brother and I would ride our tricycles around the entire block, about an eighth of a mile. It probably took us about 10 or 15 minutes. You never worried about strangers back then. Most people were good and looked out for little children. We didn't have two-wheeled bikes because we lived in the city and there was too much traffic.

On hot summer days the firemen would open the fire hydrant next to my school and all the children would put on their bathing suits and get wet from the spray. We had a lot of fun running under the water with the other kids.

One day during our first winter at Woods Place, my mother wasn't going to be home when I returned from school. I was told to ring the doorbell and my cousin, Tommy Fagan, who I didn't really know very well, was supposed to let me in. I must have stood on the front stoop for a half-hour, ringing the doorbell and knocking on the door.

It was a bitter cold, snowy day and my hands and feet were freezing. At that time, I didn't know the Mason sisters well enough to go next door. Finally Tommy, who thought it was amusing to make me wait while my hands and feet became numb, came down and let me in. This incident sure didn't make me feel any fondness for my cousin. I'm sure my mother told my aunt about it, and she never depended on Tommy for anything again.

My brother was very advanced academically, so he went to private school. For first grade, my parents registered me at Holy Cross Catholic School, which was across the street from our house. I wore a uniform from first grade through fourth, a white blouse with a peter pan collar, red tie, and a navy blue skirt. The only difference in dress from fifth through eighth grade was a navy blue tie replacing the red one. School was separated into boys and girls sections. The Christian Brothers taught the boys and the Sisters of St. Joseph taught the girls.

TROUBLE IN PARADISE

During that first Christmas season at Woods Place, my brother William went to spend the day at a friend's house, and my mother took me shopping. When we returned, Sis Pigott came over and said we looked like Santa Claus with all the packages. And then she told mother that William had been struck by a hit-and-run driver and was in Kings County hospital, where Dad was on the staff.

William was in the hospital for almost two weeks with a fractured skull and numerous cuts and bruises, and spent another week at home recuperating. I can still remember Dad telling Mother that "due to the fact that this was my brother's second fractured skull (he was born with one as an instrument baby) he wouldn't be able to survive any more traumas to his brain."

William got well and life was good until March of 1943. My brother was home with Dad and Mother and I went grocery shopping. Living in the city, we didn't need a car and, like everyone else, we walked everywhere. On the way home, my mother suddenly became ill and asked me to carry the groceries. When we walked in, she went straight to the bedroom to lie down. I put the groceries in the kitchen and told Dad that Mother was sick. He ran to her and knew she was in the midst of a stroke. He called an ambulance and sent me to the rectory to get a priest to say last rites.

While Mother was in the hospital, Father called my uncles and grandmother to see if William and I could go to the farm to spend the Easter Holidays. Off we went by bus, and Uncle Tom met us in Newburgh at the terminal.

BACK ON THE FARM

The farm was familiar to us because we spent about six weeks there every summer. Mother would always pack a picnic lunch and take us there on the Hudson River Dayline, a large ship that left from New York City. One of our uncles would pick us up at the dock in Newburgh after the three or four hour trip. It was a fun day for us.

Mother used to help with the picking and packing of fruits and vegetables. Dad would usually come for a long weekend in the middle of our stay. He always sent a large package with a ham, hot dogs, bologna and other cold cuts and goodies from Merkles or Trunz German butchers during our stays.

There was no running water at the farm. When my uncle bought it, it didn't have electricity either, but electricity was added to the house and barn shortly before Aunt Regina was married. Her wedding reception was held at the farm.

We had a pump for drinking water. We would pump a bucket at a time and bring it into the kitchen where we would use a dipper to get drinks. The water was wonderful, very cold with great taste. For laundry, bathing, and cleaning we collected rainwater in a large wooden barrel by a downspout in the back of the house. We also had a two-seat outhouse, quite "uptown." It was always very clean, and it had a bucket of lime with a scoop in it to minimize the odor. The farm was wholesome and lots of fun.

Across the front of the house was an open porch that ran the width of the house. Fresh produce was put on that porch and sold to customers who passed by. There was a door at the center of the house, and Uncle Mike's office was to the right of it, just off the entrance hallway. To the left was the green room (so named for its large green area rug) that was used to store produce.

Adjacent to the green room was a small room called Blue Beard's room. It sounds spooky, but it wasn't at all. It housed items from yesteryear, even an old wooden harp. In the back of the room was a window that faced the back hallway, which made me think the whole back end of the house was an addition. If I'm right, it was probably done shortly after the house was built. The ceiling height was different depending on which part of the house you were in.

There was a trap door leading to the basement in the back hallway, but it was never used because the steps were completely deteriorated. There was a clothes hamper on the top of the door, which was even with the floor. Jackets were hung on hooks on either side. The basement had a dirt floor where much of the packing of produce was done in colder months.

By the time my uncles owned the farm there was an outside cellar door on the side of the house. The dining room was built over a cistern that may, at one time, have supplied water to the pump at the kitchen sink, but certainly not now.

There was a door to the dining room from the green room. Both the dining room and the kitchen were in the back of the house with a hallway in between. There was an icebox in that hallway that Uncle Tom would fill during the summer months with a large block of ice. He'd pick up the ice in Newburgh and bring it home on the front bumper of his car. In the winter, there was no need for ice; we'd just put perishables on the screened-in stoop.

Both a front and back stairway (we usually used the back stairway) led to four large and two small bedrooms. One of the small bedrooms was my grandmother's and the other small one was used for storage. Two of the large bedrooms were used by my uncles, and the other two were reserved for company. The house was really neat.

The large kitchen had a cast iron stove for cooking and providing heat. If we wanted to warm something quickly during mild weather, we'd use a hot plate. There was a very large pantry closet and sink, but there was no running water—the old pump next to the sink didn't work. In the dining room we had a log-burning stove that used wood from the property (there was no coal). We spent cold weather months mostly in the kitchen and dining room; there was no heat in the rest of the house. By the time I lived on the farm, the house was well over a hundred years old.

We spent a busy week with our grandmother and uncles. In addition to the house there was a very large barn that contained a big cider press and two large, wooden vats that were each about 30' high and 20' across. I can remember how they made cider with less-than-perfect apples. The press was powered by energy from their tractor.

The apples were pressed between filters that were made of a very heavy canvas. Both the canvas and the vats had to be cleaned. Most of the cider was put into the vats, but many people came with their own gallon jugs to fill. Cider has a very short life because if kept too long it first becomes hard (alcoholic) and later turns to vinegar.

I still recall fondly that when I was eight, Mother was washing the floor of the farmhouse and had a glass of hard cider that gave her the giggles while she worked. That was probably the last time she went to the farm because she had her first stroke soon after. To run the press was a lot of work. By the time I went to live on the farm they no longer made cider.

The rest of the barn was filled with hay used for horse food and bedding. My uncles had two large workhorses: a white horse named Bill and a brown horse named, of course, Brownie. There were two large wooden-topped barrels in an enclosed entranceway between the barn and the work sheds. One barrel was for horse feed (oats, wheat and molasses) and the other was for chicken feed or corn. There were other small, detached buildings, which could be called sheds.

There was also a small smokehouse used to smoke hams. Although I don't remember seeing pigs on the farm, I know they were there in earlier years. There was also a granary where explosives were kept (used to blow up boulders that were in the way of farming) as well as fertilizer and chemicals for spraying the trees. They also had a chicken coop and a bee coop. The bees were used to pollinate the fruit trees.

We were staying at the farm after Mother's first stroke when I had a brilliant idea. Knowing that my uncles didn't have much money, my brother and I were in the bee coop and I spotted flat boxes that were used for packing the honeycombs.

I told my brother we could make lots of money for the farm by filling the boxes with wild onions from the fields. We ruined many of the boxes by filling them with the onions. Needless to say, my uncles were not very happy when they found the boxes. We got a good scolding for my bright idea.

When we left, we had no idea we wouldn't see our grandmother again. She died two and a half years after Mother.

LOSING MY MOTHER

Mother was still in the hospital when we came home. She had been in a coma for two weeks. Our next-door neighbors and my Aunt Helena took care of us when Dad was at work. When Mother finally came home she seemed fine physically but was very confused. Her personality had changed, and she had to learn to read and write all over again. She would mix up my name with my brother's. Every day, as Father would go to work, he would warn Mother not to overdo. In 1943, the only thing the medical profession did for high blood pressure was offer garlic pills and a diet.

About six weeks later, Mother had another stroke, but less severe. About a year after the first stroke, Mother and I went shopping in downtown Brooklyn. She wanted to buy an Easter hat, but had difficulty paying for her purchase. She became so upset she wasn't sure what subway to take to our neighborhood. After stopping to ask many people for directions, we finally arrived home. I think I was as upset as she was because I wasn't that familiar with downtown Brooklyn, either. She had a total of seven strokes within fifteen months and died in a coma from the last one on June 3, 1944.

Our poor mother must have had a premonition of death. One day, between strokes, she said, "Marian, I am going to teach you how to braid your hair." She took three pieces of heavy cord and tied them to the back of a kitchen chair and proceeded to show me what to do. I would part my hair in the middle and then on the side, then take the hair from the side to the top of my head and braid it. Then I would incorporate that braid into the braid I'd made on the back of my head, and tie it with a rubber band. I would take a piece of ribbon and fold that braid under and tie it into a bow. It took quite a bit of time to finish my four braids.

One day after Mother died, Father said, "Marian, I wish you would concentrate more on your teeth than your hair." I don't think he realized what a job it was for a ten year old. Another thing Daddy would do was take us gently by our shoulders, pull them back, and say, "Stand straight." He was determined that his children would have nice smiles and good posture. When I was about 11 or 12, the Sister who taught us asked me to come to the front of the classroom. I wondered what I had done. She said to the rest of the class, "I want to use Marian as an example of how to keep your hair neat and out of your eyes."

Shortly afterward, I caught head lice from someone at school. Back then they didn't have the means to get rid of them as they do today. Mary Mason would come to our house and separate my hair into sections. Then she would dip a piece of cotton into kerosene and apply it on my scalp and continue all the way down to the end of my hair.

Since my hair was long—half way down my back—it was quite a job. After the kerosene treatment, my hair had to be wrapped in a towel for a period of time to kill the lice and their eggs. Then Mary would take a fine toothed comb to my hair and wash it.

She must have worked on my hair for weeks, because my scalp was getting irritated from the kerosene. Finally, Mary said it would be easier to get rid of the lice if my hair could be cut to shoulder length. I agreed and Miss Mason—showing patience, perseverance, and love—got rid of my lice. What a wonderful person she was! I let my hair grow and then, in eighth grade, I had it cut again.

A week before Mother had her last stroke, we were in the bathroom together and she said, "Marian, if anything happens to me take care of your brother." I promised I would and, in less than an hour, she had her final stroke. A week later, at only 49 years of age, she died.

After her death, life changed considerably for us. Aunt Helena moved to an apartment about a block away. It was as though the Donovans blamed Father for our mother's death. I can remember Father saying, "At the funeral parlor, when I tried to talk to your Uncle Mike it was as if there was a brick wall between us." I was 10 and didn't see our uncles or the farm for the next five years.

Father said, "Out of respect for your mother's memory I don't want you going to the movies for a year, and there will be no Christmas tree this year." The evening before Christmas, my brother and I were walking on Church Avenue, a few blocks from home, and the merchants were closing for the holiday. I said to my brother "Let's just take a tree and keep walking." We did, and nothing was said. We put it outside the door and Dad let us decorate it. I don't think he asked where it came from, but it was there and it made a 10 and 11 year old very happy.

Being German our father was brought up Lutheran, but he was determined to raise us Catholic for Mother's sake. He sent us to confession every Saturday, whether we needed it or not. We never missed a Sunday Mass, a Holy Day or a contribution to the collection. I love the Catholic faith and it has brought me through many storms in my life. I also believe that, regardless of your religious affiliation, God answers your prayers if you follow his commandments. When it was time for my Confirmation, Dad asked me—and I agreed—to take the name Catherine, after his sister.

REMEMBRANCES OF WORLD WAR II

World War II broke out in 1941 but, since I was only seven and didn't have anyone close in the service, it didn't affect me very much. I remember sirens going off for air raids and blackouts. We had special window shades you pulled all the way down to the sill so that lights couldn't be detected during a blackout.

There were also ration stamps. You received books of stamps based on the amount of people in your family. There were red books for meat and blue books for other groceries. I remember a shortage of tea and butter. When those items were to be found, Mother or Father would buy for the future and store the butter in the freezer. There were also green ration stamps for gasoline, but since we didn't have a car we didn't get them.

When I was about eight or nine, our teacher gave each of us the name of a young man in the service who graduated from Holy Cross elementary school. My soldier was named Albert Deering, and I wrote to him the entire time he was in the army. When Albert came home after the war his parents had a welcome home party for him. He lived only a few blocks away and I was invited. I asked if I could bring my brother, and the Deerings agreed. We had a nice time.

The day the war ended I was on Flatbush Avenue, probably doing an errand for Dad. There were parades and celebrations, and people were hugging, kissing and shouting. It was something to behold.

LIFE WITH MY NEIGHBORS

The Mason sisters and Sis Pigott did more then their share for us after Mother died. Dad took the midnight to 8 a.m. shift so he would be there for us during the day. Mary Mason came over every evening after dinner when Daddy was leaving for the staff house to catch some sleep before work. Mary stayed until Father returned from work in the morning. Many nights she didn't get much sleep because my brother or I would be up most of the night with an asthma attack.

When I was 11, I became very sick with a severe case of tonsillitis and asthma just a few weeks before Christmas. It was so bad that my father put me in Kings County Hospital, where he was on staff. One of the things written on my chart was that I had a severe egg allergy, but one of the nurses brought me eggnog without realizing what it was. I drank it and became much sicker, and when Father came to visit me you could hear him all over the hospital. The little mix-up probably delayed my homecoming by a day or two. Next spring, Dad had my tonsils and adenoids removed.

Sis Pigott, a beautiful redhead in her early 40s, was a supervisor with the New York Telephone Company. But every time there was a school procession or play, she would find the time to curl my hair. I'd go next door to her large and lovely room, and sit at her dressing table as she put my hair up in rags. The next day I would go back and she'd take my hair out of the rags and curl my hair around her fingers. I would leave thinking I was every bit as pretty as Shirley Temple.

Sis Pigott and Brother Rooney took my brother and me to Rockefeller Center where Brother Rooney worked. We had lunch with them and enjoyed a tour of Manhattan. Another time, Sis took me to the telephone company to see all the operators working at the switchboards.

A little over a year after Mother died, Sis Pigott was diagnosed with rectal cancer. She only lived three or four more months and dwindled down to nothing. After Sis died, Brother Rooney started to drink quite heavily. He lost his job and the situation worsened.

One time, he sat on the porch railing and fell to the concrete steps below. He did major damage to one of his knees and had to have surgery. It didn't teach him anything and, after many warnings from the Mason sisters, they finally put him out and he became a street person.

I was a bit of an imp, I must admit, and probably got away with a thing or two. One day, my brother and I were walking past a pet store that had puppies in the window. We went in and asked how much the Heinz 57 variety puppies cost, and they were only two dollars. I really liked a cute little black puppy, but the lady said I had to have a note from a parent saying I could buy it. I didn't have the money with me, but I had a piggy bank at home with quite a bit of change in it.

We went home and counted my money, which was more than we would need to buy the puppy. My handwriting wasn't bad, even at that age, but I'm sure it didn't look like an adult's. I wrote a note saying my children could buy the puppy, signed it, and brought it back to the pet store. I think they cared more about the sale than who wrote the note. We went home with the puppy, and though our poor father didn't need any more responsibilities, he let us keep it.

My brother graduated from eighth grade at the age of 12, and by this time he could speak conversational Spanish. Our father said that sometime in the future Spanish would become the second language in the United States. Dad taught him the language and he was right; it *is* the second language in the States today. I will never understand how he knew.

The Mason sisters were always there for us. When my brother was almost 13, Dad registered him at Saint Francis Xavier Catholic High School. Dad thought it would be better if he took William to the staff house to stay over on school nights. William was closer to school there, and Dad felt he could get William off to school in the mornings. All the doctors who worked at the hospital had a room at the staff house, probably in case of emergencies, when they would be on call.

My brother wore a navy blue military uniform with a white stripe down the outside of his pant legs. I can remember father ironing those pants and using cleaning fluid on the stripes. The uniform had to be clean and pressed and the shoes shined.

When I was about 12, Father bought me a beautiful Lane hope chest. He said I should use it to save everything that was special to me until I was older. My father had a studio picture taken of the three of us about a year after Mother died. One of the prized possessions that went into the chest was that picture. Other beloved items were a doll I had won in school, an antique doll and quilt the Mason sisters had given me, a picture of a pretty young lady who I believe was Dad's sister, and my graduation group picture from eighth grade. The chest ended up at Aunt Helena's house, went into storage and eventually was lost. It was a big loss because I don't have any pictures of my dear father.

SHOPPING IN THE NEIGHBORHOOD

Father did most of the grocery shopping himself but, occasionally, my brother or I would go with him. One day I went with him during a blizzard. The snow was so deep and the wind so cold we stopped at a diner for a bowl of Manhattan clam chowder to warm up before finishing the walk home.

Every once in a great while, during the summer, Father would fix bacon, lettuce and tomato sandwiches for dinner. He would send me to Woolworth's five and ten cent store to get a pound of potato chips to have with our sandwiches.

The store had bins of potato chips that were very fresh, as well as other treats that were sold loose. There was a large metal scoop in the bin and the salesgirl would scoop what you wanted into a brown paper bag and weigh it using circular weights that would balance with your purchase. Father always got a pound because he knew my weakness for potato chips. He realized that, by the time I arrived home, only half a pound would be left in the oily brown paper bag. The chips were great and I never let Dad down; I always returned with half the chips.

There was a large German bakery, called Ebinger's, about two blocks from our home. It was actually a bakery and a distributorship. By the time the retail store opened in the morning, the trucks were loaded and leaving. You had to get there early because, even at 7 a.m., there could be 10 or 15 people ahead of you. Everything was fresh from the oven, still warm when packaged, and so good to eat.

Many times, Dad would send my brother or me to the bakery. We would get pumpernickel or rye bread for Dad and myself, and white bread for my brother. Mother had also been a white bread lady. I believe that Entenmanns's eventually bought Ebinger's and their wonderful breads, pastries, and cakes. When Mother was alive she always enjoyed a piece of jellyroll or pastry from Ebinger's with her cup of tea.

In the evenings, when Father left with my brother for the staff house, I would spend time next door on the Masons' porch, learning to knit. Then Mary would take me home and sleep over. The Mason sisters were wonderful: Mary was sweet and gentle and Annie was a little sterner, but also a great lady. Annie had a droopy eyelid as the result of a stroke some years earlier, and she was also hard of hearing. When I spoke to Annie I had to talk loudly for her to hear me. I think that's why I spoke loudly most of the time.

MORE ABOUT MY FRIENDS AND NEIGHBORS

In my mind, the Mason sisters were saints for spending so much time and energy on our family. They let me go up to the attic of their house and sort through old things they had stored there. It was really neat and very large. There was a door in the upstairs hallway with stairs leading up to it. The attic had a good-sized window on each side of the house. It also had electricity providing me with lots of light.

One of the things I found that was really great was a picture of a girl by a fountain that Annie's boyfriend had painted for her. I could see Annie's face in that portrait. When Annie died, Miss Travers took the picture and, after I was married, she had it framed and gave it to me. For many years I couldn't hang that picture because the ceilings weren't high enough. Now it hangs in our upstairs hallway in Seneca, South Carolina.

The Mason sisters washed and ironed my dresses and uniforms and even gave me birthday parties. They provided a wonderful mother image for me. Mary made a blue and white check spring coat for me on her old-fashioned sewing machine, operated by a foot pedal. The coat had a lining and pockets, and I thought it was beautiful.

The Nuns at Holy Cross Grammar School were great to me, too. Often, when they went shopping downtown, they would ask my father's permission for me to join them. When we returned, I would visit the convent and receive a treat of something delicious like hot cocoa with marshmallows.

I had a special girl friend at school, Nina Ortega, who was of Spanish heritage. Whenever there was a function at school, Dad would get in touch with Nina's Mom and ask her to take me clothes shopping. She was a stay-at-home mom and I guess he figured that since she had two girls of her own she would know about a little girl's clothes.

About the time Mother died, Ann Marie Campbell—a girl of Irish heritage who we called Cissie—was transferred into my class. Although I've lost contact with Nina, Cissie and I are still friends today, and she's the only link to my childhood. She's the only person left who remembers my father, brother and the Mason sisters.

In May of 1947, Mary Mason was invited to her cousin's ordination in Troy, New York. She hadn't been feeling well and was receiving medication for her heart. When she received the invitation she called the doctor, who advised her to "Go and enjoy the weekend."

On June 2nd the parish priest visited Annie to tell her that her sister Mary had died of a heart attack the day before the ordination. I was with Annie when she heard the news, and my heart was broken because Mary was so dear to me. The priest took me aside and said, "You have to pull yourself together for Annie because Mary was the only person she had."

With the help of Dad and Annie Mason, time passed and I started eighth grade. The school year went quickly and plans for my eighth grade graduation began. I was measured for cap and gown, and I understood why Dad always called me his little peanut: at the age of 14, I was just 4' 8" and weighed only 79 pounds.

LOSING DAD

Father was a wonderful man, firm but loving. Every noon I walked the one block from school to have lunch with him at home. It was great because we always talked and spent quality time together. He cooked balanced, delicious meals for us and was always there for us each day.

On Saturdays, Dad would take us for walks to Prospect Park where we would visit the zoo and have Cracker Jacks and Coke. Then he would buy a bag of peanuts so we could feed the squirrels as we left for home. One day I was feeding a squirrel and decided it should eat the peanut off my fingers. The squirrel thought otherwise and bit me. I tearfully learned a lesson as Dad medicated my punctured finger.

Father took us to Coney Island, Steeplechase Amusement Park, Sheep's Head Bay, or Luna Park for swimming whenever he had time. He would buy hard rolls, mozzarella cheese, and beautiful tomatoes from an Italian merchant. Dad would cut the tomatoes and cheese with a large penknife and fill the roll with them. We would get Cocoa Cola to drink with it. It was wonderful. I also remember getting homemade French fries, in a large paper cone, on the boardwalk in Coney Island. They were absolutely the best, made with fresh potatoes.

Dad and I had a wonderful relationship. Many Sundays when my brother was at a friend's house, he and I would go for long walks along Flatbush Avenue and talk.

On May 31, my brother and I were having dinner with Father, when he stood to get us seconds. Father put his hand to his heart and said, "Oh, God, no, not yet," and fell to the floor. William ran to get help and I tried to breathe into father's mouth, even though CPR wasn't known back then. Somehow I knew dear Daddy was gone; there was nothing I could do. He was 67 years old and had been my hero. I didn't know what I would do without him. The ambulance came and took his body to the morgue. It was about three weeks before my eighth grade graduation.

MY NEW HOME

I was so hurt by the way the Donovan family had treated father, I was determined not to live with any of them. I went next door to tell Annie what happened, and she put her arms around me and said, "You have a home with me, we will have each other." She and her sister Mary had almost been second mothers to William and me ever since Mother fell ill. When she offered to take me in, there was no doubt I would live with her.

My brother decided to live on Staten Island with Aunt Helena. Her son, Tommy, was out of the navy and was living at home with his mother.

After Father's funeral, I took my few belongings—including my dog and cat—and moved in with Miss Mason next door. Her house was very different from the one we had rented. Ours was smaller but had central heat; the Mason's house didn't. Instead, there was a cast iron stove in the kitchen used for cooking and heat, and also a gas stove that could be used for cooking in warmer weather. There was a beautiful isinglass stove in the dining room, basically a fancy potbelly stove through which you could see the flames.

The bathroom and all the other plumbing were in the basement, which received its heat from the kitchen and dining room. There was a small hallway in front of the basement—where Miss Mason kept her phone—and there were stairs leading to the second floor. The door at the foot of the stairs helped ensure the heat wouldn't be lost upstairs.

In the colder months, we spent time downstairs in the large basement, which was very pleasant and bright. The main floor had front and back parlors separated by pocket doors and a sewing room. The top floor contained two large and two small bedrooms.

I always thought that the house in which the Mason sisters lived was built a few years earlier than the house we rented from them. Their basement had no accommodations for a furnace. Their basement rooms had gas fixtures on the walls that were used for light in the years before electricity. Although they were no longer functional, they looked rather neat.

I got a kick out of the Mason sisters because they were very old-fashioned. For example, they kept two iceboxes in the space under the front porch. One was used to store canned goods and the other to keep their perishables cold. In those days, icemen came around and cut the amount of ice you wanted and put it in the icebox for you. The Masons had no refrigerator or electric iron, just two old-fashioned cast irons that were heated on the stove. As one iron started to cool, you switched the handle to the other iron.

Our aunts had cleared anything of importance out of 22 Woods Place, which was then rented to a young, 30-something couple by the name of Burke. Mr. Burke's sister, Mary, lived with them, and so did their two small children, five-year old Jimmy and his four-year old sister, Marian (who spelled her name the same way I did).

I had a good summer. Miss Mason was kind enough to let me keep my pets. My dog, Blackie, made the transition from an inside to an outside dog. Annie had a little dog house built for the side yard. My cat, Poody, was an inside/outside cat but spent most of his time outside. Miss Mason sent me one block away for swimming lessons at Erasmus High School, the school where Father had taught languages.

In the fall I went to Catharine McAuley Catholic High School. I wore a uniform that consisted of a maroon jumper and yellow blouse. To get there, I had to walk a few blocks, take a trolley, and then walk a few more blocks.

My grade-school friend, Cissie Campbell, also went to Catherine McAuley, but we didn't have any classes together. She took commercial courses and I took academic courses, so we didn't see each other at all. There was a different order of Nuns—the Sisters of Charity—who taught at this school, and they were also great to me.

LOSING ANNIE MASON

During the first week of November, Miss Mason became ill. Like her sister Mary, she suffered from a heart condition. Annie had to spend about two weeks in the hospital (not the one where Father had been on staff) and I had to take a trolley to downtown Brooklyn to see her. Although my memory is vague, I believe I lived alone in the house during her hospitalization. But I felt quite safe because I had my dog and the Burkes were within hollering distance.

Helen Travers, a woman 10 or 15 years younger than Miss Mason but a very close friend of hers, was Annie's legal executor and handled her affairs while she was incapacitated. She and I made up a beautiful Murphy bed for Annie in the rear parlor of the first floor. When not used as a bed, it stood upright and appeared to be a cherry wood bookcase. We placed a commode near the bed so that Annie would not have to move around a lot.

Annie came home by ambulance on the Friday before Thanksgiving. She announced that "Marian and I are going to live like queens." And she asked Helen to "Call the lawyer. I want to change my will today." Miss Travers said, "It can wait until Monday when you will have lots of time." I would soon learn that you shouldn't put off things that require doing. Saturday went fine, and I brought Annie things to eat and drink and we spent time together. On Sunday morning, November 21, I checked on her to be sure she was okay. She was asleep and I left for 9 a.m. Mass.

I met Cissie at Mass and walked her halfway home afterwards. As soon as I returned home I went to see Miss Mason, but found her dead. I couldn't believe it was less then six months since Father died and only about a year-and-a-half since Mary Mason's death. Annie was a kind, loving person and now she was gone, too. I blamed myself for not coming straight home from church and went next door to ask for help from the Burkes. Mrs. Burke said, "Come back to 22 Woods Place and live with us, Marian. You can help with the children."

Helen Travers was invited to a Thanksgiving cocktail party and dinner at a friend's penthouse apartment on Madison Avenue. Since the Burkes already had holiday plans, Helen asked if she could bring me along so I wouldn't be alone. That was so very kind and thoughtful of her.

When we arrived at the large and beautiful apartment, it was filled with guests I didn't know. I was a little shy, so I found a place to sit on the corner of a couch. A waiter came by and gave me a glass of wine, a beverage I had never tasted before. I drank it and had quite a struggle to walk from the couch to the dining room. After dinner I was fine, but I wondered why people would drink something that made their legs feel like rubber.

THE NEXT
STAGE OF MY LIFE

I didn't know anything about caring for children, but I decided to take the Burkes up on their offer. They gave me the bedroom my brother used to have, and didn't ask me to do much. Occasionally, I took the children—who were very cute and well-behaved—to the movies. And I really loved them.

Mrs. Laura Burke was a full-time homemaker who was pretty and nice. I'm not sure what her husband, James, did for a living, but he seemed like a nice man, as well. They were very good to me, and I stayed busy commuting to and from school and studying.

I don't remember what became of my cat and dog. My guess is that Miss Travers probably had the ASPCA pick them up since there was no one to care for them. At that point I was too busy trying to get my own life in order to worry about my pets.

For a while, I wondered why God was treating me this way, why he would let so many people die who I loved. I guess one could say I was feeling sorry for myself. I knew I needed motherly and fatherly guidance and protection, and I prayed to Jesus and his mother Mary for help. I knew God would be there for me, so I went to daily Mass whenever I had time.

Today I look back and my life makes more sense to me. We couldn't take care of a sick father, and the Mason sisters wouldn't have been able to care for a child if they weren't well. It was an honor knowing and being loved by such wonderful people. There is a reason for everything and if we do right, God is there for us. I think that problems in life draw us closer to God and make us stronger and more considerate of others. Everyone has problems sooner or later.

Miss Mason left her property—two houses, garages, a barn and a roofer's workshop—to Holy Cross Church, which was my church. Her money and all proceeds from the sale of household antiques were left to the Propagation of the Faith (for the poor). Helen Travers talked to the priest and he agreed to give me free tuition at Catherine McAuley High School for the four years I would be there.

So many people showed me kindness. For example, Steve, the roofer who rented the shop behind Miss Mason's house, knew that my parents didn't have a headstone. He made a beautiful 3' x 2' copper cross and asked the Todds—an older couple who rented a garage from Miss Mason—to drive me to the cemetery so I could put it on my parents' graves.

The Todds drove me all the way to Long Island, but the cemetery wouldn't let anything be placed on the graves other than a traditional headstone. We stood the cross in a vacant lot in the cemetery and never told Steve; we didn't want his feelings to be hurt. When we returned to Brooklyn, the Todds took me to their apartment and treated me to homemade apple pie and tea.

A CHANCE
TO BE ADOPTED

Miss Travers screened everyone who wanted to look at antiques in Miss Mason's house. When she wasn't able to take people through the house, she called the Burkes and I'd do it for her. After Thanksgiving I took a couple, Mr. and Mrs. Salmon, through the house. They called Miss Travers later, and when asked what they were most interested in, they said, "The little girl who answered the door and showed us through the house."

The Salmons, who were in their 40s, had been married a long time but couldn't have children, and they were interested in adopting me. A date was set for me to spend the week between Christmas and New Year's Day at their home in the Bay Ridge section of Brooklyn. I was very impressed when they took me upstairs to what would have become my room. They had been using it as a den, and it was quite large. It also had a television. It was 1948 and it was the first TV I had ever seen.

Mr. Salmon had a management position with ConEd, a utility company in Brooklyn. Mrs. Salmon was a homemaker and baked cookies with me. She gave me some, but I was too shy to tell her about my egg allergy, and I was afraid I was going to become sick. I got around it by putting back the cookies she gave me when she wasn't looking.

They were a very nice, attractive couple. Mrs. Salmon took me shopping and bought me a skirt, blouse and my first lipstick. They had a little dog, Foxy, that would dance around the living room on his hind legs and do tricks. While I was there, they had a holiday party, giving me the opportunity to meet their family and friends.

I had a wonderful week with them but I didn't want to be adopted. I hardly knew the Salmons and I had been through so much in such a short time. I worried about my last name being changed, and I didn't want that to happen because I loved Dad so much. That was probably silly because when you marry your name changes anyway. The Salmons may have thought I was ungrateful, but I didn't mean to be. I really liked them.

ON THE MOVE AGAIN

Because I was shy, I took small portions of food at dinner so I wouldn't be a financial burden to the Burkes. By March, I had lost quite a bit of weight and Helen Travers made a doctor's appointment for me. The doctor told her that I should go to live with relatives. She called my Aunt Helena who said that she, her son Tommy, and my brother would come and get me on the last Saturday in March. My jobs were to tell the Burkes and notify my school that I was transferring to New Dorp High School on Staten Island.

I loved the Burkes and didn't have the heart to tell them I was moving away. My solution was to pack my suitcase and have my friend Cissie waiting in the back yard to retrieve it as I threw it out of the window. Of course, it never occurred to me that anyone would wonder about my disappearance. Anyway, we carried out my plan, but Mr. Burke saw Cissie catch the suitcase and demanded to know what was happening. Needless to say, I didn't leave the Burkes on very good terms. I still feel bad about it because they had been so good to me. Honesty is the best policy and I should have mustered enough courage to tell them.

Aunt Helena's home, a two-bedroom cottage she purchased on a shoestring, was small but comfortable. She was always on the lookout for other small homes in the neighborhood that needed attention. If one was for sale and the price was right she would purchase it, clean and paint it, then sell it as quickly as possible and pay down her mortgage with the profits. Aunt Helena did this at least two or three times.

I only went to my new high school for two-and-a-half months and I hated it. It was very large and I didn't know anyone. It was late in the school year and everyone had their own friends. As soon as school ended for the summer, my brother and I were sent to the farm in Newburgh. I loved the familiarity of the old farmhouse and barn.

LIVING ON
THE FAMILY FARM

When I went to live with my uncles I was given what had been my grandmother's room. It had a single bed, bureau, and an old-fashioned dressing table in it.

My uncles didn't waste any time giving us chores to do. The farmhouse needed to be painted and my brother and I were assigned to help Uncle Tom with that project. We learned how to make paint by mixing white lead (They should hear the reports on lead paint today!), linseed oil and turpentine. It was to be painted white with green trim.

Aunt Alice came to help for a week. One afternoon, Uncle Tom took her, my brother, and me to the grocery to shop. I sat in the back of the car with our aunt, and William sat in the front seat with our uncle.

We were near the icehouse in Newburgh when Uncle Tom had a seizure. Thank God my brother was in the front seat, because he grabbed the wheel and put his foot on the brake, stopping the car. I didn't know my brother understood how to drive but, apparently, he knew enough. He kept us from going into the lake. Aunt Alice was a nurse and helped revive my Uncle. After a brief rest period, we continued the trip to the store.

In the middle of August, William went back to Staten Island to get ready for school. When Dad died the previous year, my brother was finishing his junior year. However, Aunt Helena wasn't very strict, and William went from having a very organized life to doing as he pleased. He didn't always go to class and didn't pay much attention when he did. He was supposed to graduate in 1949, but had to repeat his senior year. He went for a few months, then quit and got a job. Eventually, he earned his high school diploma through a GED program, and found a better job at a bank in Manhattan.

Now I was alone with my two bachelor uncles. Both were modest, extremely quiet, and very good to me. My grandmother had taught them well: they made their beds every day and put their dirty clothes in the hamper. Uncle Mike went to 9 a.m. Mass every Sunday at St. Josephs Church in New Windsor. He always sat in the same pew and put his fedora (dress hat) on the windowsill near the pew.

The farm was less than a quarter of a mile from Epiphany College, a seminary for young men studying for the priesthood. The college, which was an easy walk from the house, had a beautiful chapel in which a 7:30 a.m. Sunday Mass was conducted.

Uncle Tom and I would occasionally go to Church at Epiphany. One Saturday night my friend, Shirley Rampe, stayed over and went to church with me there the next morning. During mass, Shirley said something that made me laugh and I couldn't stop. The nuns who worked at Epiphany sat behind us and I could hear one of them say with disgust, "That Donovan Girl." That comment brought me back to reality. Back then everyone knew me as the Donovan girl because I lived on the Donovan farm. The only people who knew me by my right name were my teachers and schoolmates.

Some years later, Epiphany College was closed because fewer young men were going into the priesthood. Most of the property was sold to the Newburgh Board of Education and is now a middle school. The rest of the property on Route 32 was sold to builders who created condominiums and shops. It was a beautiful piece of property and it still is, in a different sort of way.

FARM LIFE
WAS NEVER DULL

Uncle Mike, the older of my two uncles, was 58 and a politician. Tom, who was 47, had a twinkle in his eyes. I was able to speak more openly with Uncle Tom, and we would tease each other. He had a drinking problem, although it never interfered with his work. He was always up early and didn't drink until his farm work was done.

When I lived in Brooklyn I had a piggy bank that looked like an old-fashioned radio with a speaker in the front. If I removed the speaker I could take money out of the bank. There were candy stores just a few blocks from our house where I could buy penny candy or an occasional candy bar. I didn't have the luxury of walking to a store in the country, and I didn't have the money to waste either.

Uncle Mike sat in an easy chair every evening, listening to his 3' high radio. On weekday evenings, from 7:30 p.m. to 8 p.m., I listened to *The Lone Ranger* with him. On Sunday afternoons, around 4 p.m., we listened to *The Shadow*, which featured the voice of Lamont Cranston. Mr. Cranston, who was a friend of Uncle Mike, lived in the Rock Tavern section of New Windsor, and owned a large turkey farm there.

Uncle Mike kept a cookie tin filled with gumdrops, orange slices, and other candies, next to that easy chair. I wasn't really that interested in Uncle Mike's candy, but sometimes I'd eat a piece. One day while I was dusting, I had a real craving for chocolate and I found what turned out to be ExLax. I ate a few pieces and satisfied my craving, but I soon paid the price. I didn't have any great chocolate craving after that and haven't had ExLax since.

Now as I look back, I realize Uncle Mike was probably scared having a 15-year-old niece dumped in his lap. He was strict and wanted me home by 9:30 at night, and demanded good grades on my report card. I was an average student, but he felt that 80 should have been 85 and 85 should have been 90.

The back of the farm was at the foot of Snake Hill, so called because of the number of snakes that came down the hill. Shortly after I moved to the farm, Uncle Tom and I were walking in the fields near the side of the house when he put his hand on my arm. There was a rattling sound and he told me not to move. He had been carrying a pitchfork, and he swung it into the ground. Then he showed me the rattlesnake he had killed. There were lots of snakes on the farm, including copperheads, garter and black snakes. In the hot, dry weather they would come down Snake Hill looking for water.

Our neighbor, Dr. Boccar, had a big brick house that sat back from the road. He also owned acreage behind him on Snake Hill. He decided to sell the house in which he and his family were living and use the other acreage to build a new house with a pool and a horse barn. It didn't take long for the Boccars to have a terrible time with snakes. They ended up putting in an electric fence to shock the snakes and keep them out of their pool.

A few times when I went to pump a bucket of drinking water, a snake would be on top of the wooden platform I needed to stand on. I would bring the empty pail back to the kitchen and leave it up to my uncles. I hate snakes. I always felt that they mesmerized me. My uncles didn't want the poisonous ones around but they liked the others because they kept the rodents down.

It sure wasn't Brooklyn

Before school started in the fall, Mr. Stenglein, a farmer friend of Uncle Mike's, rode by with his daughter, Loretta, who was a year younger than me. They were going to hay at another nearby farm. Back then, haying was quite a job; there were no balers like today.

The hay was cut by a five or six-foot blade that was attached to the side of a tractor or, in some cases, a contraption pulled by workhorses. The blade reminded me of giant electric hedge clippers. The cut hay was left in the fields to dry, and it was turned occasionally with a pitchfork. When the hay was completely dry—which it had to be because if it was stored damp, it could cause a combustion fire—it was gathered with a large hay rake pulled by a tractor or horses, and then pitched into a hay wagon to be taken to the barn.

When the Stengleins stopped by, my uncle introduced me to them. Loretta said, "My brother and I go to square dances and they're fun. The next time we go dancing we'll invite you."

When my brother left for Aunt Helena's, my uncles and I worked the fields. We picked and weeded tomatoes when we weren't painting the house. I really didn't mind working in the tomato fields because Uncle Tom would fill a gallon jug with well water and I would take a salt shaker with me so I could salt the tomatoes. I ate them like I would an apple. They were delicious off the vine.

Our uncles had three Russian Samoyeds, medium sized dogs. When their puppies were about three or four weeks old, I helped wean them from their mother. That was done with a saucer of warm milk and very small pieces of white bread soaked in the milk. You just put the puppies' little snouts in the milk and they got the idea to lap up the milk and bread. The puppies were so cute with little floppy ears and curly tails. When the puppies were ready, they were sold: $5.00 for the females and $7.00 for the males.

The adult Samoyeds were watchdogs. Each was tied to a doghouse on different sides of the house. Two of the three were females: Yen Yen and Snookie. Roscoe was the only male. Snookie was old and Roscoe was mean. When I fed the dogs I would always put Roscoe's dish out of his reach and push it toward him with a stick because there were times he would try to bite me.

Sundays were our day off. We went to church, ate dinner at noon, and had afternoons free. During many of those Sunday afternoons, I would sit near Yen Yen, talk to her, then take her for a walk around the farm. There were two ponds where I loved to watch the frogs frolic.

Near one of the ponds was an abandoned still that remained from prohibition days. It had actually been the foundation of an old abandoned house where some of the farm help lived, long before my uncles owned the property. The farm was 98 acres so there was never a problem finding a place to walk. After my walk I would sit in the sun by the barn door and study. It was very pleasant and wholesome.

Making chicken (and beef) soup

A funny thing happened the first weekend I was alone on the farm with my uncles. On Saturday, Uncle Tom brought a headless chicken into the kitchen in an oval dishpan. He said, "From now on, you'll be the chief cook and bottle washer in this house." I had never cooked anything in my life! Dad was always afraid I'd get burned. The most I ever did was wash the dishes, dust a little, and run errands.

The chicken had all of its feathers still attached. I looked at Uncle Tom and asked, "What about the feathers?" He set the dishpan down in the sink and poured boiling water from a kettle over a section of the feathers. Lo and behold, they came right out. "Now," he said, "you have to get all the feathers out, even the pinfeathers, and any hairs that may remain. When you're finished, rinse it good with cold water and put it in the icebox."

The following morning, I was to get up early, put the chicken in a large pot of water with a half dozen chicken bouillon cubes, and add chopped vegetables, rice and noodles. The soup—about as hardy a meal as you could want—was to be ready at noon for Sunday dinner. And it was, or so I thought.

When Uncle Mike took the chicken out of the pot to carve he said, "This chicken isn't clean." I replied, "It sure is, there isn't a pinfeather or a hair on it." He said "What about the insides?" "What insides?" I asked. The dogs ate pretty well that week and we settled for canned corn beef and Campbell's soup. I learned how to properly clean the insides of chickens and did all right after that.

Homemade soup was our main meal Sunday through Wednesday, and sometimes Thursday, too. One week would be chicken, and the next week beef. The beef was a roast that Uncle Tom would pick up at the market. Basically, I would follow the same recipe. There wasn't a lot of time to fuss with cooking on the farm. There were too many other chores.

One Sunday morning when I was fixing soup, I became distracted and went outside. I must have been gone quite a while because when I came back, the stove and the flue pipe were bright red. I doused the fire with water and I was lucky I didn't burn the house down. But I ruined the soup.

I took the beef out of the pot and cut off the burned part. Then I drained the liquid, added more bouillon cubes and boiling water, and salvaged whatever vegetables in the pot I could. I really sweated that one out. My uncles never said a word even though the soup tasted burnt. And I learned a very valuable lesson: Turn the flue down before leaving the house. I was always very glad they didn't see how red the stove had become. It really scared me.

Another job I had was collecting eggs and feeding the chickens. I was a little afraid that the chickens would peck me so I would always chase them off their nests to get the eggs. My uncles never knew, and I don't think they would have approved if they had.

COUNTRY FUN

There was an old two-wheel bike in the barn that must have been Tommy Fagan's at one time. I had never ridden a two-wheeler, so I practiced in the barnyard for a while before taking it out on Union Avenue, a rarely traveled road built on a hill.

I climbed on and was almost to the foot of the hill when a milk delivery truck started to come towards me. I applied the brakes but nothing happened, so I jumped from the bike into the ditch at the side of the road. I wasn't hurt, but I picked up the bike, walked it back to the barn, and never got on again.

I started going to square dances with the Stengleins and I loved it. The dances were from 8 p.m. until 11 p.m. My uncles didn't mind as long as I was with the Stengleins. Sometimes I'd stay over at their house after the dance. Uncle Mike allowed me to stay there because he knew the Stengleins so well. The friendship between my uncles and the Stenglein brothers went all the way back to when they were young men.

Soon after I moved to the farm, my friend Cissie Campbell and her whole family came to see me. Cissie's father parked the car on the road and I went out to greet them. I felt funny about inviting them in because I didn't feel I had the right to do so. They came a long way and I should have been more considerate. Mrs. Campbell teased me for years about not being invited in, even for a cup of tea.

When I got to know my uncles better, I relaxed a bit. Occasionally one of the Rampe sisters (more about the Rampe family later) would stay over and my uncles didn't seem to mind. Loretta Stenglein could never stay because her family ran a dairy farm and she and the other children had to get up early every day to help with the milking.

After Labor Day, school started. I always felt lucky that the farm was in the upper Cornwall school district. The school grades were kindergarten though twelfth grade. I was starting tenth grade, which had about 30 students. My friend, Loretta, was in ninth grade. When I started, I switched from academic courses to commercial. I was in school a few days when I realized it was up to me to make friends. My uncles were rather quiet men and I knew I needed other people in my life.

COUNTRY WORK

An amusing thing happened that fall while I was finishing painting the house. We were in the back of the second level, where the lower roof had a little slant to it. I was high on the ladder and Uncle Tom was holding it so it wouldn't slip.

We were almost finished when Uncle Tom said, "Would you mind if I went down to the foot of the hill (there was a bar there) for a beer?" I told him to go ahead but, within just a few minutes, the ladder slipped. I fell on my chin and all the paint that was in a bucket atop the ladder spilled over me. The next morning my chin was swollen to three times its normal size and it was black and blue. Uncle Mike was mad at Tom when he found out what happened and worried what they would think at school. But nothing was ever said.

I don't think Uncle Tom got much more than cigarette money from Uncle Mike for his labor on the farm. As I said, he liked to have a few drinks and sometimes brought home a bottle of hooch. One afternoon I was in the front yard and along came Uncle Tom with a burlap bag over his shoulder. He was heading toward the old car he used to drive into town. (When I say old, I mean old! It had to be cranked.)

Uncle Mike came to the front of the house and said "Tom, what's in the bag?" With that, Uncle Tom dropped the bag into the trunk of the car, and replied, "Nothing." And then we heard a cluck. Uncle Mike opened the trunk and pulled out the burlap bag which had a live chicken in it. Uncle Tom had planned to barter it in Newburgh for some drinks. Uncle Mike let the chicken go and Uncle Tom disappeared.

One of my chores was to wash clothes. We had an old wringer washing machine, but no running water. There were two oval copper tubs that I placed on our cast iron stove and filled with rainwater. A reservoir was also attached to the stove, which held about another 10 gallons of water which we also used for washing dishes and ourselves. I would plug in the washing machine and add pots of hot water from the tubs and reservoir until it was filled. Then I'd add soap powder and the clothes and let it agitate.

When the clothes were finished they had to be put through the wringer. The soapy water had to be siphoned from the machine, dumped, and refilled with clear water to rinse the clothes. Then they were put through the wringer again. This was an all-day job because the clothes then had to be hung out on the line to dry.

In the winter, clothes would freeze on the line and become as stiff as boards. I'd bring them in and hang them inside to dry. Sometimes my uncles ended up with blue and red blotches on their long underwear because I didn't always separate the clothes. They didn't seem to get upset about it. At least they had clean clothes that smelled good.

Fall was the time of year for picking peaches and apples. I would come home from school, get into jeans and a shirt, and get on a ladder and pick fruit. One afternoon, I was picking peaches and decided to take a big bite out of a beautiful peach. I looked down and half a worm was left in the part I hadn't eaten. I didn't eat peaches for a very long time again. I really didn't like picking peaches because the fuzz from the peaches got on my skin and made me itch.

A few times when both my uncles would be going out for the evening I was asked to feed the horses. They were large workhorses and I was always afraid they might side step and trample me. I had to get past them to fill their trough with feed and hay and make sure they had water. As large as they were, they were very gentle and I never had a problem.

I was only in Cornwall High a short time when the Rampe family moved into the area. Mr. Rampe was the foreman of Forgehill Farms, a dairy farm near Route 94 where St. Helena's Convent and the Schoonmaker development are today. Mrs. Rampe was a stay-at-home mother. They had four children, a boy and three girls. The boy was a senior who went to Cornwall High for only about a month before returning to his old high school in Long Island.

The girls were: Anita, who was my classmate; Shirley, who was a year behind me; and Joan, who was about three years younger than Shirley. I became very close with the family; sometimes they must have thought they had four daughters. We're still friends today and our children know Shirley's children quite well since they all grew up in the Newburgh area and we visited each other often.

I had three wonderful years in Cornwall High School. The school was small enough so that the teachers knew my situation and tried to guide me as parents would.

SLEEPING IN AN UNHEATED FARMHOUSE

I had never been in the farmhouse in winter until I moved there in the fall of '49. There was no insulation in the walls. The only heat in the house was the cast iron stove in the kitchen and the stove in the dining room. We always had a very large woodpile that we used for heat. We didn't have coal to bank the stoves with. Even if we put large logs on the fires before we went to bed, by morning the fire was usually out. Upstairs, the bedrooms were always cold in winter. If it was 20 degrees outside, it was the same inside.

Before I went to bed, I'd take two hot bricks from the kitchen oven, wrap them in a towel and put them under the covers at the foot of the bed to keep my feet warm. Usually the bricks (and my feet) were cold within an hour. In the winter I wore underwear, a flannel shirt, jeans, a sweater, and socks to bed. The bed had many covers and a quilt on it.

In the morning, while my uncles were doing their chores in the barn, I would run down to the kitchen. I always hoped there would still be a fire in the stove but, many mornings, I had to get one started. I'd brush my teeth, wash with water that wasn't very warm if the stove was cold, and get dressed. I look back now and realize it wasn't that bad. In a way it was kind of fun, like camping out. I had a home and people who cared about me, and I appreciated that.

Sometimes the wood heat would aggravate my asthma and I would go outside and sit in the cold air on the side porch until I could catch my breath. One night I was so sick with asthma that Uncle Mike got scared and at 10:30 p.m. went to an all-night drugstore in Newburgh to get medicine for me. It turned out that I was a late bloomer: when I turned 17—my senior year of high school—I went through puberty and my asthma condition disappeared,

You have to be motivated to be a farmer. There's more work than meets the eye. My uncles, for example, were up and out every morning by 6 a.m. to feed the horses and clean the stalls. There was fertilizing, tilling, planting, spraying and pruning of trees to be done. Equipment had to be sharpened, oiled, and in working order. Being a teen-ager, I would say the percentage of work I did, compared to my uncles, was very small.

We had a hand-dug well that wasn't very deep. Late every summer the well would run dry and, every three or four days, Uncle Mike would go to the waterworks in New Windsor to fill two or three large milk cans with water. Between the animals and the humans we went through quite a bit of water.

AUNT HELENA COMES FOR CHRISTMAS

Uncle Tom and I would pick out a nice tree on the property before Aunt Helena arrived for her annual Christmas visit. He'd cut it down and we'd carry it back to the house. Then he'd help me decorate it with bubble lights and lots of decorations from years past.

I usually had the turkey ready with mashed potato stuffing and all the trimmings. (I wonder what it would taste like to me today?) Uncle Mike even bought plum pudding for himself and Aunt Helena. The pine scent from the tree and the home cooking must have put Aunt Helena in the Christmas spirit. I look back now and think she really went out of her way to come up to the farm at that time of year.

Many times, Aunt Helena would call me Regina (which was the name of my mother's youngest sister). One day I asked her why, since we didn't look anything alike. She said, "Because you both are pleasers," which I took as a compliment. I'm not sure that some of our children would have agreed I was a pleaser, especially during their teen-age years. I had always admired my Aunt Regina because she was pretty and had a nice disposition.

Auntie Travers (Helen Travers) was also very good to me. I think she felt somewhat responsible for me after Annie Mason died. Before Labor Day and again before Christmas, she would send a box of clothes to me with skirts, blouses, and other items I could use for school. Shoes were a problem because they had to be sized properly. Auntie Travers never mentioned shoes, and she probably never thought about them. I would never ask her for anything because she didn't have to do anything at all for me. And I managed.

When school started in the fall of '49, my shoes didn't look too spiffy. After all, I had used them for working in the fields and painting the house. I found a pair of my grandmother's size seven (my size) white dress shoes that had never been worn. I painted them with liquid brown shoe polish and put brown laces in them. They had to be repainted quite often because the polish constantly wore off. No one ever seemed to notice since no one ever said anything about them.

After Christmas, I was going to visit Aunt Helena in Brooklyn. I had saved some money and, on the way there, I was going to buy myself a pair of penny loafers in downtown Newburgh. Uncle Tom dropped me off at the Newburgh bus terminal, and I can still remember dragging my suitcase the few blocks to the discount shoe store.

But the price was right; you could buy good shoes for less than $3 back in the late '40s and early '50s. Money could go pretty far back then even though the paychecks were pretty small.

During the three high school years I lived with my uncles, Auntie Travers sent me two beautiful winter coats. She also sent me $2 every month, and I was very careful how I spent it. I would put a little in the collection basket every Sunday. I would buy an occasional lunch at school or an ice cream cone at a little candy store I could walk to in Cornwall. A peanut butter and jelly sandwich was my usual school lunch. The rest of the money was saved for necessities like shoes or snow boots.

Uncle Mike didn't see much sense in a girl going to school past 16 years of age. There were many pocketbook factories in the Newburgh area and he was sure it wouldn't be difficult for me to get a job. He had only gone to school until he was 14 and did very well for himself. He owned the farm and had been in town politics for years. First he was Justice of the Peace—a job he held so long everyone referred to him as "Judge"—and, in later years, Road Superintendent. Times had changed though, and Aunt Alice insisted I graduate from high school. She got her way because she subsidized the farm. A short time after her discussion with Uncle Mike she had a serious stroke, but he kept his promise to see me through high school.

Aunt Helena cared for Aunt Alice after the stroke, and Alice lived with her for about a year-and-a-half. She was partially paralyzed on one side and was affected mentally. Despite her paralysis, she walked to the local police station one day while Aunt Helena was at work. She decided to turn herself in for something she didn't do. Aunt Alice walked about a mile, crossing main intersections, and could easily have been hit by a car. That was when Aunt Helena realized she could no longer leave her alone and would have to put her in a nursing home.

JUNIOR PROM NIGHT

I occasionally had crushes on boys, but I was quite shy and didn't bother much with them. It was Junior Prom time in the spring, and Miss Travers sent me a beautiful gown to wear. I didn't have a date yet, but about a month before the big event, Anita Rampe said her boyfriend Tony would fix me up with a blind date and I could go double with them. Since I had the gown, I agreed.

We decided to go to the movies a couple of weeks ahead of time so I could meet Jimmy Rose, my prom date-to-be. We made arrangements to pick him up at the Newburgh Savings Bank. As we neared the bank, I saw a fellow standing there who was chewing tobacco and spitting. Jokingly I said, "I sure hope that's not him." It was! I went to the movies with him that night and to the prom, as well.

On prom night I was to stay at Anita's house. For the entire date, Jimmy Rose kept telling me how much he liked me, and I said, "I'm older than you," thinking that would discourage him. He said, "Age don't make no difference, not when you like a person." After the prom, I couldn't wait to get from the car to behind the Rampes' screen door so I didn't have to kiss him goodnight. I ran as fast as I could and slammed the screen door shut as he came up on the porch. Not a very happy memory of the Junior Prom!

SENIOR YEAR IN HIGH SCHOOL

During my senior year, Upper Cornwall High formed its first football team. There was lots of excitement, with a rally and bonfire planned. One girl from each class was to be selected as a representative at the rally. Cheerleaders were the best-looking girls, but they were excluded to give the more "average" girls a chance. Much to my surprise, I was chosen as the senior class representative.

A few months later, a really beautiful girl transferred into the senior class. Her father was an officer who was assigned to West Point. If she had been there earlier, I think she would have been chosen to represent the senior class, hands down. After the rally, the team and cheerleaders marched through town, and the girls chosen to represent their classes rode on the backs of convertibles in a parade through town. It was a fun evening!

I was also always given the job of collecting money for class events. One fellow in our class said, "You never leave us alone until we pay up." Obviously that's why they gave me the job. Later in the year I was chosen as the friendliest girl in the senior class, and that made me very happy.

In the fall we had a senior class play, *Where's Laurie?* My friend Anita Rampe and I tried out for it and we were delighted to be chosen as part of the large cast. I played the role of a cheerleader named Maddy. We had a great time, and it gave me confidence in myself.

Generally, I didn't have any difficulty getting home after rehearsals. With football season in full swing, there was a late departing sports bus. But one afternoon the bus didn't show, leaving me and Warren Miller—a classmate who was also in the play—facing a nearly 10-mile hike home to New Windsor.

Warren asked me if I'd like to walk with him and I was happy for the company. We were about halfway, when a man stopped and offered us a ride. Warren accepted, but with a condition: the man had to take me home first, which was about three miles or more out of the way. I always admired Warren for showing such respect for me. We probably should never have taken the ride, but the man who offered it turned out to be a good person. You wouldn't dare do that today.

Time passes quickly when you're busy. I went to school, kept house, helped on the farm and managed to get to New York City a few times. Aunt Helena would buy round trip tickets for me to take the Shortline Bus. I'd get on at the foot of the hill near the farm, and Aunt Helena would meet me at Port Authority Bus Terminal in Manhattan. During Christmas vacation, she would take me to Radio City to see the Rockettes and then we'd go to Chinatown for chow mein.

CHILDHOOD DISEASES STRIKE

About a month before graduation, my friend Anita stayed overnight with me. (In all the time I was at the farm I can only recall Anita or Shirley spending the night with me.) We slept in one of the larger bedrooms and talked and laughed until we fell asleep. We had planned on catching the school bus the next morning, but when I awoke I had a bad sore throat and felt terrible. I told Anita she'd have to get the bus by herself.

After the bus left, large welts broke out all over my face and body. It turned out to be chicken pox and I had it from the top of my head to the bottom of my feet. It was in my mouth (that's why my throat was sore), ears, scalp, even between my toes. I worried about Anita catching it since we slept in the same bed. I called her house but Anita's mother said not to worry since Anita had chicken pox when she was much younger. I was out of school about a week and went back with a few tell-tale scabs.

The following year, when I was working, I started to feel awful again and went to the doctor. He smiled and said I had measles. He also said there wasn't much you could do about measles, and warned me not to kiss my boyfriend! I thought I had had measles as a child, but it must have been German measles. I couldn't believe I was getting these childhood diseases in my late teens.

GOING TO THE BIG CITY
TO WORK AND LIVE

Graduation time came. Helen Travers sent me a beautiful, formal gown to wear when I went out after graduation. Aunt Helena made the trip to the farm and went with Uncle Mike to watch the ceremony. They were quite proud of me, especially when I was given an award for being the most improved senior. Aunt Helena gave me money to go out with my friends afterwards. I didn't have a date, but neither did lots of the graduates. So we all went out together and had a great time.

I always had it in my head that when I graduated I would return to the city—where I could live with Aunt Helena—and get a job. Aunt Helena had recently sold her home in Staten Island and bought a house in Porter Corners, a tiny hamlet off Route 9, outside of Saratoga, New York. The house had originally belonged to Helen Travers' sister and brother-in-law, and Helen sold it, completely furnished, to my aunt. But Aunt Helena also rented a small efficiency apartment in Manhattan, and agreed I could stay with her.

I left the farm to live in New York City, and soon found a job as a file clerk with the Atlantic Insurance Company on Wall Street. I worked from 9 a.m.-5 p.m. A mid-day meal was included, and the food was great: soups, sandwiches or dinners. But our offices were in the center of the building and there were no windows. Just about the only time I saw daylight was on the way to and from work. I guess I had become a "country girl" because I truly missed the light of day and the fresh air of the Newburgh area.

On those occasions when I got out of the building, it was to go to the bank or run an errand—and the crowds of people reminded me of a cattle stampede. I may not have been fair about this because, after all, it was Wall Street, the financial district of Manhattan (and, probably, the world). I was so used to living in the country, I hated not being able to see daylight. And I didn't like my job.

You really can't go back and expect everything to be the same. And this was Manhattan, not Brooklyn. When you think of New York City, you always think of Manhattan even though it's only one of five boroughs. Manhattan is known for high-rises and sky-scrapers, which make us think, "city." Brooklyn is one of the five boroughs and, like Manhattan, it has many sections or neighborhoods within it

For example, there is Bay Ridge, Coney Island, Green Point, and Flatbush, to name just a few. I grew up in Flatbush, and I think one of the tallest buildings in that area was the six-story apartment where I spent the first six years of my life. Flatbush was comprised primarily of single-family homes, attached homes, and some apartments.

GOING BACK TO THE
FARM TO LIVE AND WORK

Manhattan is a great place, but I think I was looking for a connection to my past. After a few months, I asked Aunt Helena if she thought Uncle Mike would let me go back to the farm and I could get a job in Newburgh. She suggested I call him, and he said, "Okay."

At the time, I didn't realize Uncle Mike was serious about a woman who would one day become my Aunt Frieda.

When I returned to Newburgh I had no success finding work during the first few weeks. I finally went to an employment agency to which I agreed to pay two weeks salary to find a job for me. They made it relatively painless by taking a half-week's salary, before taxes, for the first four weeks.

They found a bookkeeping position for me at the Grand Union Tea Company, a warehousing operation that made home deliveries of non-perishable groceries and housewares. I did disbursement sheets, payroll, and other numbers-related tasks for five-and-a-half days each week. I earned the princely sum of 98 cents an hour plus overtime. And that wasn't too bad in 1952. I loved my work and was always busy.

MY FIRST CAR

The spring after I returned to the farm, I had a call from Joan Keller, a friend who had been a year behind me in school. She said her grandmother, who was in her eighties and living on Long Island, was giving up driving. Joan asked if I would be interested in buying her grandmother's gray '48 Ford coupe for $500. She told me it had low mileage and was in great condition.

I took driver education in high school and passed only because of the kindness of my teacher. He told me to "Marry someone who knows how to drive. You will never get a drivers license." The problem had been that I had no automobile to practice on at home.

I knew it would be great to have a car because I had to walk a half-mile to get the Shortline bus to Newburgh. Then I had to catch a local bus to Dupont Avenue and South Street. The trip back and forth to work was over an hour each way, but would only take about 15 or 20 minutes by car.

I didn't have a driver's license but thought I could teach myself to drive on the farm. I had the money for the car because, before Father died he had opened accounts for my brother and me, and there was $700 for each of us. I told Joan I'd buy it and, just a few weeks later, her parents drove her to Long Island to get the car and drive it home to me.

On many Sunday afternoons Mr. Stenglein, a very patient man, tried to help me synchronize the clutch and gas pedal on the South Street hill. One day, while practicing driving in the fields, I somehow got the car stuck on a tree stump. I asked Uncle Tom for help, but after a number of tries he finally decided, "We'll have to tell the Judge (Uncle Mike)." That was a fate worse than death since Uncle Mike didn't believe I needed a car.

It took a lot of work, but my uncles got the car free. I decided on the spot to call Davis Driving School. I made arrangements for Mr. Davis to pick me up during my lunch hour at work. After many weeks of practice I took my driver's test and passed. It was wonderful having my own transportation, and what a great little car it was. I even drove Aunt Helena to Porters Corners a few times.

Joan Keller's mother called me after I bought the car and told me that when I needed gas or service I should go to Jimmy Pep's Gulf station on 9W in Newburgh. She said he was an honest man and would do right by me. I did as she told me and she surely was right.

I had the car for nearly a year when, one day while going to work, I realized I had hardly any gas. I was riding on fumes but didn't have any money, and wouldn't until payday. I stopped at Jimmy Pep's and asked if he would do me a favor and let me have two dollars worth of gas until the end of the week. He said "absolutely not." I must have had a look of horror on my face, but he was teasing me. He laughed and said, "I'll fill it up, and there's no hurry paying me."

Joan Keller had graduated from high school in 1953. She was planning to go to college in the fall but, along with Loretta Stenglein, took a waitress job for the summer at Hill-Mar Lodge in Washingtonville. Joan asked if I'd be interested in waitressing on weekends, and I thought it would be great. I'd get to work with my friends and earn a little extra money.

I bought a few white waitress dresses and aprons for my new job, but I really wasn't very good at it. I was there just a few weeks when I spilled coffee on one of the guests. He was a very nice young man and told me not to think anything of it. I decided to give my notice before I was fired. I gave the waitress dresses to Loretta, because she was about my size. She later took a job as a dental technician, so the dresses received plenty of use. For years, I kept one of the aprons from that job as a remembrance of the experience.

DINING WITH
MR. TRAPINI

I had three managers at Grand Union Tea Company. One of them was Mr. Trapini, a first generation Italian, probably in his mid-40s. He was a very nice man, and very much a family man. He was married to a lovely little Italian lady, and they had three children: a 16-year-old girl and 12-year-old twin boys.

On Secretary's Day, Mr. Trapini took me to lunch at an Italian restaurant in Newburgh. I ordered a salad that was full of olives and many other goodies. I was 19, and trying to act very sophisticated. After the salad was served, I put my fork into a black olive, but I hit the pit, making the olive bounce in the air, off the table, and onto the floor. I was mortified. Mr. Trapini smiled and said "Marian, pick up the olives with your fingers."

Mr. Trapini's wife invited me to a real Italian dinner at their home in the neighboring town of Maybrook. As I left the office it was snowing, and as we were eating, the snowfall became heavier. When we finished, Mrs. Trapini said "You can't leave. It would be too dangerous to drive home in this weather."

The Trapinis had a small house and, needless to say, I didn't have any pajamas with me. Since I was about the same size as their daughter, Patty, it was decided I could wear Patty's pajamas and share her double bed. She was a sweet girl and didn't mind. When I called my uncle to tell him I wouldn't be coming home and that I was staying over at my boss' house, he wasn't happy. The next morning I followed Mr. Trapini to work.

FINDING NEW RELATIVES

I was back on the farm about a year when Uncle Tom died quite suddenly. Uncle Mike said he died of alcoholism, but I always felt it was the result of seizures. The Donovans were all prone to strokes and seizures. Out of respect for Uncle Tom, Uncle Mike delayed his planned marriage to my soon-to-be Aunt Frieda.

At Uncle Tom's funeral I was surprised to learn that my grandmother had a brother, Mike Lynch, as well as a sister, Catherine Sharp, both of whom lived in Newburgh. They had had a falling out with Uncle Mike and hadn't been in touch for years. Uncle Mike had brought both families to Newburgh, and both worked on the farm for a short time.

My Uncle had high expectations for farm workers and, apparently, the Lynches and Sharps didn't live up to them. As a result of stubbornness on both sides, the relationship terminated. It's so sad that things like this happen to families; we've seen it happen a few times ourselves. I really didn't put the whole story together until I visited my cousin in Ireland and learned more about the family. Aunt Regina's sons, Bill and John Anderson, were quite helpful in charting our ancestors.

Our Irish relatives didn't know about the alienation. They always thought the Lynch sisters (my grandmother and her sisters) were extremely close. If circumstances in my life had not led me back to the Donovan family I would have lost my relationship with my mother's family. In a way it was a blessing. We all have to learn forgiveness.

My husband Tom went to Saint Patrick's High School with Vernon Sharp. Vernon's grandmother was Catherine Sharp, my grandmother's sister. When we went to Saint Patrick's 50th reunion, Vernon had already passed away. Mary Lynch, Mike Lynch's granddaughter, was a speed ice skater in Newburgh. Mike Lynch was my grandmother's brother. It is a small world!

GETTING TO KNOW AUNT FRIEDA

My future Aunt Frieda was a widow with two daughters. I knew both girls from Cornwall High School: Dotty was two years ahead of me, and Jean was two years behind. Uncle Mike and Frieda were married in the fall of '54 in St. Patrick's Church in Newburgh.

Tony Marshall, Uncle Mike's politician friend from New Windsor, was the best man and Aunt Frieda's daughter, Dotty, was matron of honor. The wedding was quite small; in fact, Jean and I were the only guests other than the wedding party. The luncheon was at the Palatine Hotel, followed by a return to work! I know for a fact that Aunt Frieda went back to the farm with Uncle Mike, where they changed into work clothes and picked apples for market.

Before Aunt Frieda married Uncle Mike, she had the entire house renovated. God bless her, it was necessary. I'm sure some of the money used to restore the house was hers. She had the foundation fixed, built a garage, dug a well, and added plumbing and central heat. A modern kitchen was installed and the small upstairs storage room was turned into a bathroom. Hardwood floors were put in throughout the house and insulation was blown behind all of the walls.

In most old farmhouses there's a problem with rodents and we had our share. Miraculously, Aunt Frieda got rid of all the critters. Many times while I lived there, I could hear them scurrying around at night and would cover my face with the blankets. As if that did a lot of good!

After Uncle Mike was married, he decided to sell 96 of the farm's 98 acres. He kept only the farmhouse, new garage, and the two acres surrounding them. When Uncle Mike gave up farming at the age of 63, taxes increased so much he didn't have a choice but to sell. He had put in a lifetime of hard work.

A building contractor, Mr. Warmer, expressed interest in acquiring the property. Aunt Frieda said Mr. Warmer had agreed to pay $55,000 for the 96 acres, and came to the house to have Uncle Mike sign the papers. Aunt Frieda left them in the dining room to attend to something in the kitchen. When she returned in just minutes, Mr. Warmer had talked Uncle Mike down to $50,000. Aunt Frieda said to me, "Your uncle isn't a businessman."

Mr. Warmer's son died in an accident the following year, and I believe the property was then sold to another contractor. Only a small portion of the farm has been developed to this day, including a children's play park on the end of the property going down the hill off of Union Avenue. The farmhouse is still standing, but the current owners had to remove the front porch because the road was widened so much the porch was almost on top of it. The barn, sheds and coops are long gone.

My next car

I had my Ford about three years when Joan Keller's mother called again. She asked about the car, and I told her it was great. But she thought it was getting old, and suggested that I go to Courter Chevrolet in Washingtonville during their sale on new 1956 Chevrolets. Courter was a very small dealership, basically a garage that fixed cars and had two new autos on display inside the garage. (There was no showroom.) The 1957 Chevrolets had already come out and they needed to sell the cars from the previous year.

I agreed that it was a good idea to take a look. I drove to Courter's and saw a black and white Two-Ten and an aqua Bel-Air. I fell in love with the Bel-Air, but the Two-Ten was $1700 and the Bel-Air was $2200. I never liked to get deep into debt so I chose the Two-Ten and the dealer gave me an allowance of $500 on the Ford coupe, which is what I had paid for it.

By this time, I was working at a bank. I decided that since I was no longer required to work on Saturdays, I'd get a second job and pay off the car sooner. I became a checker at the Grand Union Grocery, which was owned by the same company where I had been a bookkeeper, but it operated under different management.

I worked one evening a week, plus Saturdays, until the car was paid off in about a year. In those days, there were no conveyer belts in checkout lines; you simply pushed the groceries with your hands. Between counting money at the bank and grocery store, I developed dermatitis (my skin split) on the fingers and palms of my hands. When I would check out customers at the store and accidentally hit the corner of a box with my injured hands, it really hurt. I tried over-the-counter salves but they didn't help.

One day I told Mrs. Keller about my hands and she suggested that I see a doctor in Washingtonville who was very good with skin problems. I made an appointment and obtained a prescription for an ointment. I used it for a short time, and it completely cured my problem. I was so relieved I wrote the doctor a thank-you note.

Working at the grocery store meant I didn't have a lot of time for socializing, but I enjoyed my co-workers and the patrons. And it was all worth it to have the car paid off.

Marian's mother, Mary Donovan, in the 1920's

Marian and her brother, William, on the Donovan family farm in
New Windsor, New York . . . about 1938

24 and 22 Woods Place, Brooklyn, New York . . . about 1940

Marian's Uncle Mike (Donovan—maternal uncle)

Lottie and Al Chaleff

Marian, Mrs. Cohen, George and Gale

Tom and Marian on their wedding day, March 1, 1958

4 Rocky Lane, New Windsor, New York—Our first house

Gilligan family reunion, June 1, 1968 (Kim's 5th birthday)

Jeff's 1st birthday with siblings and myself—June 13, 1968

Chippewa on Brant Lake, Chestertown, New York

House in Holly Creek, Anderson, South Carolina, 1979-1997

Tom and Marian on 35th Wedding Anniversary, March 1, 1993

House in Cross Creek, Seneca, South Carolina, built 1997

House in Boca Grande, Florida, bought in 1997

Tom, Marian and children, Gilligan family reunion, August 2003

Tommy, Lettie and family, Patrick, Meggan, and Jayson

Bob, Ainslye and their boys, Christopher and Bobby

Kathy, Fernando and their boys, Matias and Frankie

Kim, David and family, Madison, Carson, and Dylan

Jeff, Tammy and family, Addie and Jack

ON THE MOVE AGAIN

Aunt Frieda owned a home in Cornwall, and Uncle Mike asked me to live there with Aunt Frieda's daughter, Jean, until it was sold. They didn't want Jean there alone. At the time, Jean, who worked as a school secretary in Cornwall, was going with the man who would become her husband.

I moved in, picked up after myself, and helped with the dishes. But Jean's hours were more conducive to starting dinner, which was usually ready when I got home from work. She also cleaned the house on Saturday mornings when I was at work. Months passed by and there were no buyers for the house.

The day before Mother's Day, Jean called me at work and scolded me for working on Saturdays. She said I was only working so I wouldn't have to help with housework or Mother's Day dinner. I could never do anything right in her eyes, and I started to cry when she hung up. Harold Colvill, the warehouse manager at Grand Union Tea Company, and a man old enough to be my father, said, "Marian, you're 21 years old. Leave and rent a room."

On the way home, I stopped at the Stengleins and told them my dilemma. They said that Lottie Chaleff and her mother, who lived just up the road, wanted to rent a room in their house. Mrs. Stenglein called them on my behalf, and asked her daughter, Loretta, to accompany me there. I liked Lottie and her mother immediately, and they said I could move right in. I went to the house in Cornwall to pack. No one was home, so I left a note and moved out.

Uncle Mike and Aunt Frieda were furious with me. They had Jean move in with them rather than wait until the house was sold, which finally happened a few months later. One day I got a welcome call from Aunt Frieda, who said, "I can't blame you for moving out. Jean can be very difficult at times."

One Saturday the following winter I was working when, much to my surprise, Jean walked in the door. She told me she was getting married in a few months and wanted to know if I would be in her wedding. I told her I'd love to. We stay in touch to this day. Jean is fine now; I guess we've both grown up.

LIVING WITH
A NEW FAMILY

Lottie Chaleff was about ten years older than me and was married to a very nice man, named Al. They had a five-year-old girl, Gale. Lottie, her mother (Mrs. Cohen), and her family were very good to me. They would insist I eat with them if I were there at mealtime. They were Jewish so I ate things I never tried before. I only paid $15 a week for the room, but since that didn't include meals, it made me feel guilty to eat with them. I would often go to the diner or grab a sandwich at a deli and eat it in Downing Park. Sometimes I would take Gale with me to run errands, and sometimes we'd go ice-skating. It was like having a little sister I really enjoyed being with.

One day, Mrs. Gledura, a route salesperson who worked for Grand Union Tea Company, came into the office to see me. She said, "You're a young girl working with all these older men. I'm interested in having your job." She explained that her daughter worked at Newburgh Savings Bank where there was a job opening. Mrs. Gledura said that if I was hired for that job, she'd ask for mine with Grand Union.

I interviewed with Mr. Smith, the bank president, and I was hired. He said one of the main reasons he gave me the job was because of my height (all of 5'5"). I could be seen above the teller window. It was funny because he was extremely short. I gave two weeks notice to Grand Union and trained Mrs. Gledura as my replacement. Switching jobs was probably one of the best things I could have done.

About the time I went to work at the bank, Lottie became pregnant and had a little boy, George, who was five years younger than Gale. He was named after Lottie's brother who had been killed in a motorcycle accident. I baby-sat for both of them quite often.

One Saturday, Lottie's other brother Lester, his wife, Paula, and their daughter, Nadine, came from New York City for a visit. Lester had a single engine airplane he kept at a small airport nearby, and was looking for someone to go up in the plane with him. Lottie and her mother said, "Marian, go up with Lester, you're always helping us." I finally agreed and had an enjoyable couple of hours. We flew over the house and he pointed out places of interest from the air.

The following Saturday, while I was attending a wedding, Lester visited again with his family. This time he took Lottie's husband, Al, for an airplane ride. When I returned from the wedding, Mrs. Cohen and Lottie were running up and down the driveway, crying and screaming. They had just received word the plane had crashed and Al and Lester were both killed.

I had just flown with Lester the previous week and I realized how easily it could have been me. It was a sad time. Two young, healthy men left families behind. Al and Lester were buried in New York City and I baby-sat for Gale and George so Lottie and her mother could attend the funeral.

Soon after the tragedy, Mrs. Cohen asked if I would share her room so she could rent the one I had been living in to the couple who owned the restaurant/bar across the road. I had no problem since there were twin beds in the room and I'd also have my own bureau. For what I was paying, I couldn't complain. During Mrs. Cohen's life she would lose her three children, including Lottie, who died of cancer in the mid-'70s from cancer, when she was only 51. They were all wonderful people.

LIFE MOVES ON AND
I MEET TOM

I had male friends, and I enjoyed going to the movies and square dances. I met a young man at a wedding who asked me to go on a movie date. He seemed nice, and we had an enjoyable time. On the way home, he told me he liked me, and asked me to come to a family picnic next weekend. Meeting his family after a first date was a little too fast for me. I barely knew him, so I told him I was busy. I was enjoying independence and a commitment-free life.

At work, I was in charge of the school savings department, which revolved around 22 schools. What a coincidence when I found that my Uncle Mike also worked for Newburgh Savings Bank; he picked up the school savings bags at the various schools and delivered them to the bank. I had no idea we were fellow employees!

School Savings bags were brought in Tuesday mornings. The passbooks were posted on Tuesdays, Wednesdays, and Thursdays and returned to the schools on Fridays. I had an assistant who pulled the matching bankcards to each of the passbooks and helped post them. There were no computers in those days; the postings were done on a National Cash Register.

Each school account was balanced, passbooks put back in the appropriate canvas bags, and corresponding cards re-filed. One of the girls hired to help in the department was Pam Mallarkey, and we worked well together. She was at the bank a short time when she became engaged to Ira Conklin, during the Christmas of '56. That became important to me because her fiancée had a friend named Tom Gilligan.

Pam and I were together at the local diner when a group of young fellows came in. She pointed out Ira, who was with Tom. That Easter, Pam asked if I would double date with her and Ira. My date was to be Tom, who was on spring break from Providence College. I wasn't doing anything and said I would. We met Tom and Ira at the Aragon, a local bar where young people got together. We had a nice time and then Tom went back to college.

ANOTHER TERRIBLE FAMILY INCIDENT

Early in May of 1957, Mrs. Cohen woke me about 2 a.m. The local police had obtained my address from the bank. My brother William, who was living at a rooming house on Staten Island, tried to commit suicide by slashing his wrists.

The Newburgh police told me to go to the local precinct near my brother's rooming house. The police would show me where to go to pack my brother's belongings and settle any debt with the proprietor. They would also direct me to Richmond Memorial Hospital, where my brother was a patient. How could anyone try to take such a precious gift as his or her life? Mental illness is very difficult to understand

I had never driven in New York City before and was a bit apprehensive. But I guess we all do what has to be done. The following day I took off from work and drove through the city to the Staten Island Ferry. That was one of the saddest days of my life.

Within a few weeks, my brother was transferred to Bellevue Mental Hospital in Manhattan. When I came home after visiting William, Lottie and Mrs. Cohen could tell how upset I was. Visiting him at Bellevue was what it must be like to visit a person in jail. I sat on one side of a window, he on the other side, and we spoke through a metal mesh partition.

Lottie said that during my next visit, she would go with me. I told her only close relatives were allowed to visit. She said, "Well now you have a sister." When we arrived at the hospital, the guard said to Lottie, "You don't look anything like William." Lottie responded, "Did you ever hear of the milkman?" She was funny, and always knew just the right thing to say.

Lottie and her mother were wonderful, caring people. Shortly after our visit to Bellevue, William was transferred to Rockland State Hospital. I was grateful because it was only an hour from home, and a much easier drive. I visited every Sunday afternoon and I could visit him alone. He wasn't confined to the building and we could stroll through the grounds. I told very few people about my brother's suicide attempt. I was so ashamed, I told the people at work he had been in an accident.

Thinking back, I hadn't seen William regularly since that summer at the farmhouse in 1949, when he left to work in New York City. The only times we met after that were a few weekends a year when I visited Aunt Helena on Staten Island. In my senior year, she sold her Staten Island house, which is when my brother moved into the rooming house.

William and I corresponded by mail and he sent me a little Christmas gift every year until I graduated high school. About a year before his suicide attempt, he got in touch and asked if he could visit with me. I was happy to have him, and Mrs. Cohen said he was welcome to stay on the pullout couch in the living room.

Lottie's family belonged to a swim club and Al suggested that my brother and I join them there. We had a nice afternoon, and Mrs. Cohen invited us to stay for dinner. I really didn't know what to do with him in the evening but decided to take him to the stock car races. He seemed very unhappy and on edge, and I thought it was because we had grown apart over the years. Al later said "Marian, don't worry. Sometimes brothers are like that." But I knew he was just saying it so I wouldn't worry.

GETTING TO KNOW TOM

Tom Gilligan came home to Newburgh after his college graduation. He called and asked me out, and made me laugh during the difficult times with my brother. I always saved Sunday afternoons for William, who was now known to his doctors as "Bill." After a few months, Tom asked if I'd let him accompany me to the hospital. He said he worried about me driving there by myself. I agreed, and we continued to visit my brother weekly.

One evening, a few months after I had been seeing Tom, he came to the house and Lottie said, "Tom what are your intentions with Marian?" I almost fell through the floor. I think his exact words were, "My intentions are to take her to the movies." Most people were very protective of me after my parents died, and Lottie was even more so after the experience I had with my brother.

On September 7, 1957, Pam and Ira were married, but I was in my friend Joan Rampe's wedding on that same day and time. Tom was Ira's best man, so we spent the afternoon going back and forth from one reception to the other.

Tom had taken ROTC in College and had a military commitment to report to Fort Benning, in Columbus, Georgia, the first week in March of 1958. Tom asked me to marry him and go with him. He was a handsome fellow, but he won me with his kindness. He was a good friend and a wonderful support for me during my problems with my brother. Needless to say, I said yes.

The first time I met Tom's parents was a Sunday breakfast at his home. His mother was so excited she burned his father's oatmeal. I discovered that Mom had actually stopped at the bank to check me out, but she mistook one of my co-workers for me.

During one of the first dinners I had at Tom's house, I took the top off the Worcestershire sauce to make it easy for Tom's dad, who was paralyzed on one side from a stroke. I had no idea you had to shake Worcestershire sauce before using it. Dad had just come home from work, dressed in his white shirt and tie, when he sat at the table and proceeded to shake the bottle of sauce.

"Who the h— took the top off?" he demanded. I sheepishly admitted it was I who had done it. Tom's brother, Mike, and Mike's family were there, and everyone started to laugh. I was embarrassed but their laughter made me feel better. And even though Dad's shirt had brown spots all over, he laughed, too.

Preparing for Marriage

The fall before we were married, Tom and I drove to Long Island to visit my parents' grave. There was no headstone or marker, and Tom said, "Before we're married let's get them a gravestone because we probably won't have the money later." We did, and he was right. We didn't have much money after we were married.

When I lived with my uncles, I usually went to St. Joseph's Church in New Windsor. But after Tom and I were engaged, I started to go with him to St. Mary's in Newburgh, where we planned on being married. While we were preparing the paperwork for our marriage, I realized I didn't know where I had been baptized. I had received First Communion and Confirmation at Holy Cross Parish in Brooklyn, but I had to research my baptism site. How's this for a coincidence: I finally discovered that I was baptized in the same church where we were to be married! And I learned that my grandmother was my Godmother and Uncle Mike was my Godfather.

When I told my friend, Shirley Rampe (her last name was now Burger), I was to be married, she said I could borrow her beautiful wedding gown and veil. Her sister, Anita, altered the gown for me and did a wonderful job. What great friends! Anita later married a fellow from Aiken, South Carolina, who was stationed at Stewart Air Force Base, outside of Newburgh. When he retired from the service he and Anita settled in Aiken, where he started a nursery business. Aiken is only a few hours from Anderson, so in recent years, Anita and I have been meeting half way.

Tom and I had a wonderful wedding at Saint Mary's, on March 1, 1958. Uncle Mike gave me away. Our reception was at the Hotel Newburgh. We kept the costs down by having a wine toast, pitchers of beer on the table, a cold plate and, of course, wedding cake. Tom and I paid for everything ourselves, including the reception. The only "outside" contribution was $100 that Tom's parents gave us so we could afford the hotel over the less upscale Monterey Restaurant. (Today, the hotel is a disaster and the Monterey Restaurant is gone.)

Pam Conklin was my maid of honor, and the bridesmaids were the three Rampe sisters and Loretta Stenglein. My friend Cissie was expecting her first child momentarily, so she couldn't come. But my friend Nina came from Brooklyn, along with Auntie Helen Travers and my Aunt Helena.

LIFE AT FORT BENNING, GEORGIA

Our honeymoon was our trip to Fort Benning. All the second lieutenants who had been sent there for training lived in the same housing development, just off base. A few weeks after we settled into our little home at 12 Mathison Road, I decided it was time to look for work.

A bus that went into Columbus, Georgia, ran along the main road outside the development, about an eighth of a mile from our house. When I stepped on the bus for the first time, I walked to the back and everyone started to holler at me. "Only niggers sit in the back," they yelled. "You sit in the front." I couldn't believe what I was hearing. I learned that blacks also had to use special water fountains and toilets. Such discrimination!

Since I had bank experience, that's where I went for a job. But when they found that Tom's commitment at Fort Benning was for only three months, they weren't interested. Instead, I became involved with the other officers' wives helping at base functions.

Everyone was in the same boat and about the same age, so we made some good friends there. After about six or seven weeks I got a virus I couldn't seem to shake. I finally went to the doctor and found that my "virus" was a pregnancy! We were expecting a Christmas present—our first baby—about December 5. Neither of us could believe it. We wanted a large family, but we never thought it would happen so fast.

Our home, which was government housing, was furnished. It was small and comfortable, with a tiny kitchen, dining area, living room, two bedrooms, and a bath. A small amount was deducted from Tom's salary to cover housing costs. Like us, none of our friends had much money, so we and three other couples rented a washing machine. We drew straws to see who would have it in their home. Once a week, all of us would meet at the "winner's" house and do our wash. Then we'd come home and hang the wash out to dry.

There was an Officers Club and a pool on base. Most mornings, Tom left the house at 5:30 a.m. As the weather heated up, he'd be dismissed anytime between noon and 2:30 p.m. Our afternoons were spent at the pool, swimming and playing cards with our friends. After dinner, many of our evenings would include a walk to Joan and Dick Mills' house. They were our friends, but they also had a TV set and we didn't. Tom always said I looked like a rabbit on our walks to their house because I'd always be chewing on a carrot or celery, which seemed to help with my nausea.

Most Saturday evenings we went to the Officers Club for dinner and I'd order a whiskey sour before dinner. (Back then we didn't know it was harmful to drink while pregnant.) By the time the meal came I was usually too sick to eat, but we chalked it up to my pregnancy. Later, we found that a whiskey sour contained egg whites, which always gave me an allergic reaction.

It was very hot in Georgia. We had an air conditioner in the living room, but it didn't begin to cool the apartment. And bugs could be quite a problem. Fort Benning was the first place where I had ever seen a roach. I found a floor wax at the commissary (military grocery) that had a bug killer in it. I scrubbed the tile floors and then waxed them.

One evening toward the end of our tour I was making hot dogs for dinner. I knocked the pan onto the floor and the hot dogs rolled out. I picked up the pan, rinsed off the hot dogs, and put them back in the pan. We were on a limited income, so we had them for dinner.

That night Tom woke up running a fever. He was very sick, and I just knew the hot dogs must have poisoned him. Early the next morning, I drove him to the military hospital on base, and he was quickly admitted. I cried all the way home. Later that day I went to visit him and found that he had blood—not ptomaine—poisoning. He had scraped his elbow crawling under barbed wire, gotten dirt in it, and it became infected.

During one of my visits to the hospital ward, I brought Tom the candy orange slices he loved. I sat on his bed so we could talk while he was eating the candy. The head nurse came along and told me to get off the bed. "Ladies do not sit on their husband's beds," she said. I was shocked, because we weren't doing anything wrong. Tom said, "Don't worry about her. She's nothing but a frustrated old maid."

Tom ended up in the hospital for nearly a week. He got out in time for the final week of his tour of duty. We couldn't wait to finish training and return to Newburgh. I cleaned for about a week because you couldn't get your retainer back if the apartment failed inspection. We had no problem getting our money.

We packed our few possessions for Uncle Sam to ship to Newburgh, and were ready to drive home right after Tom's graduation. He was to train troops in Fort Dix, New Jersey, but there was no housing there for wives. I stayed with his folks until he finished in the fall of 1958.

RETURNING TO CIVILIAN LIFE

Shortly before we came home to Newburgh, Mom & Dad Gilligan bought a new television because the old one wouldn't hold the channel—the knob kept slipping. The television was on the front porch waiting to be given away, but Tom asked his parents to keep it until we were able to find an apartment.

Meanwhile, we heard of an apartment at 361 Third Street that would be available in November. The people who were living there were friends of Tom's brother and sister-in-law, Mike and Dianne, who arranged for us to see it. It was a lovely upstairs apartment with 22 windows. I borrowed a sewing machine from Anita Rampe, bought plenty of material and got busy making curtains. I think my constant sewing almost drove Mom & Dad crazy. Dad said I had "curtainitis".

Tom couldn't get home every weekend, but I managed to see him and stay on base for some long weekends. We wrote to each other two or three times a week and spoke on the phone occasionally. In the meanwhile, Mom & Dad Gilligan were very good to me.

Tom had hoped to make the service a career but, at that time, the Army didn't need additional manpower. So he joined the Reserves and, later, the National Guard. When he left Fort Dix at the end of September, he had to find a job. It didn't take him long: After a search of just a few weeks, Eastern Acceptance Corporation, a company that financed and insured automobiles, hired him. In addition to his office work, Tom also had to repossess cars. There were many evenings when he went out after dinner to do that part of his job. I was always worried that someone would shoot him.

NEW NEIGHBORHOOD, NEW FAMILY MEMBER

On November 1, 1958, we moved into our apartment. We decorated it and hung our many curtains before Tommy was born. We had a living room, dining room, small kitchen, bedroom, and baby room, but there wasn't a lot of furniture. One of Tom's jobs between college graduation and the army had been delivering furniture for a retailer. The man who owned the store gave us a great discount, but we still couldn't afford much.

For the baby's room, we borrowed a crib from Mike and Dianne. And we bought a small, unfinished chest of drawers and painted it. We put Mom and Dad Gilligan's television in our living room and solved the slippage problem with a roll of scotch tape we kept on the console. Whenever we changed the channel we'd put a new piece of tape on the knob to hold it in place. We used that television for the two-and-a-half years we lived in the apartment and for our first few years on Rocky Lane. It took a while until we were finally able to afford a new one. But we felt we were set.

I went into the hospital the evening of December 14, 1958, and Tommy was born the next day, at 4 a.m. He was a beautiful, eight-pound boy who would drain two 2-ounce bottles at a time. It was unbelievable! We didn't go home from the hospital until December 22 because I had a problem with my blood count. When we arrived, the apartment looked so beautiful. Tom had completely decorated it for Christmas.

We had Christmas dinner in the apartment. Mom and Dad brought over a turkey with all the trimmings, and Mom made everything in our kitchen. Dinner was great and the company was wonderful. Mom was quite a help during that first week home. She came over every morning until I got back into the swing of things. Tommy was an easy baby to take care of, and was loved so much by all of us.

With a new baby, there was always plenty of laundry, and I hung our wash on a clothesline we strung between the baby's room and a telephone pole. But in bad weather, our wonderful landlords, Dot and Lennie Cavicchio, allowed us to use their dryer. The Cavicchios were probably 10 years older than us. They had three children: Leonard, 6, Chuck, 5, and Karen, 3.

Tom's grandfather, Pop, lived only three doors from us. He would walk most evenings to his daughter-in-law's for dinner (about a block-and-a-half from us) and then stop at our apartment on the way home to watch television. His wife had died years before and he was alone, so we were company for him. Pop was a wonderful man, with lots of personality, who loved to tease everyone.

Almost every day, I would meet Shirley Rampe Burger—who moved into an apartment about two blocks from us—and we'd walk our children together. At the time, she had Jackie, a 2-year old, and Terri, who was three-and-a-half months younger than Tommy. The Burgers later had two more children: Stevie, who was about a year younger than Bob, and Lori, who was about a month younger than Kim. Lori and Kim became friends as they grew older, as did Stevie and Bob.

LOSING AUNT HELENA

Tommy Fagan, Aunt Helena's son, called me on March 18, 1959, to tell me that his mother had died a day earlier, on her way home from the St. Patrick's Day parade. I thought Aunt Helena would find humor in the fact that she didn't pass away until after the parade. She was only 62 years old.

I loved my aunt, but Tommy wasn't one of my favorite people. He asked if his mother could be buried with my parents. I wondered why he didn't buy a burial plot for himself and his mother with her insurance money, and then he said he wasn't going to spend money on that. There was only enough space for three at my parent's gravesite and I wanted to save the space for my brother. But I finally agreed because of my love for Aunt Helena. I told Tommy never to contact me again.

When I told Uncle Mike about Tommy calling about the grave, he said, "He should have called me. There's plenty of room in the Donovan plot." I think Tommy didn't call Uncle Mike because he was trying to do something shifty and he was afraid of Uncle Mike's wrath.

Baby Number Two
MAKES AN APPEARANCE

About the middle of April, I started to feel sick again and found we were going to have another baby in December. I cried because I thought it would take Tommy's babyhood away. I was completely wrong about that because when children are really close, they are great companions for each other. It actually makes it easier for them growing up.

Helen Reid, one of Mom's cousins, had heard we were going to have an addition to our family. She called and asked if we'd be interested in another crib. We were delighted because, with the babies so close in age, we'd need two of them. When the time came to put Tommy into a bed, Mike and Dianne needed their crib back because they were expecting again (Dennis). Things really had a way of working out for us.

Tom had to go one night a week to the Reserves or National Guard, plus he had to give up two weeks every summer. When he went on his two-week tours, Tom's cousin, Angela Bannan (with whom I had worked at the bank), would stay at the apartment with me at night so I wouldn't be alone with the babies. She was always great company.

When Tommy was 10-1/2 months old, I had an appointment with a photographer to take his picture. As I walked down Broadway pushing Tommy in his carriage, I bumped into Pop. I told him what I was doing, and he insisted on accompanying us and buying Tommy his first pair of shoes.

We stopped first at Fogarty's Shoe Store and then had Tommy's picture taken. Pop stopped to visit with a friend he met on the walk, and I headed home. On the way, I stopped to visit my sister-in-law, Dianne. As she offered me a cup of coffee, Tommy stood up, lost his balance, and fell backward. He was fine, but as I reached down to pick him up my water broke.

Mike drove Tommy and me home. I called the doctor and he advised me to get to the hospital as soon as possible. I told him that was crazy because the baby wasn't due until December. But I did as I was told and went that afternoon. Our second son, Bob, was born at 1 a.m. on October 30, 1959, six weeks early.

When he was born, Bob weighed 5 pounds 13 ounces, and when we brought him home he weighed 5 pounds 7 ounces. A photographer at the hospital wanted to take his picture, but I said no. He was so early he didn't have eyelashes or fingernails. We thought he looked like a little plucked chicken.

We were told to feed him every three hours and to flip him on the bottom of his feet to make him stay awake and suck. The first couple of months were a little rough. It seemed that no sooner would he finish his bottle than it would be time to change him and start all over again. The extra feedings, however, paid off in a few months. Bobby filled out to be a beautiful baby. As he started to mature, I realized that God blessed us with a little boy who resembled my Dad in looks and personality.

Tommy didn't walk until he was 20 months old, but Bob started to walk when he was 13 months old. For a period of time, I had to carry both boys up to the apartment after a walk. Fortunately, our landlady would always watch out for me. If she was home and saw me with the boys, she would come out of her apartment and carry Tommy upstairs.

In addition to using our own diapers, we had a diaper service for about six months after Bobby was born. I wanted to get Tommy potty trained as quickly as possible to do away with the expense of the diaper service. When Tommy was about a year-and-a-half, I started potty training. I'd wipe up the mishaps with paper toweling and flush it down the toilet. I didn't know paper towels would clog up the plumbing.

Soon, all the plumbing in the house began to back up. Our landlord and his brother-in law dug up the sewer line and found all my paper towels. Mr. Cavicchio asked me very nicely not to put paper towels down the toilet again, and I didn't. Tommy was trained before he was two.

Cousin Pete and Pop

BECOME A BIGGER PART

OF OUR LIVES

Tom's cousin, Pete Bannan, was home from college and drove to our apartment in his VW bug. "I know what I'm going to do with my life," he announced to us. "I'm going to become a priest." Tom and I laughed because Pete always had a girlfriend and a preference for partying.

A few days later, when Pop was visiting, he asked what we had to say about Pete's decision, and we told him we thought Pete was kidding. Needless to say, we soon found out he wasn't. Tom, the kids, and I always enjoyed Pete's visits. He was always a lot of fun, and he still is, even though we now think of him as Father Pete.

Pete often brought special treats for the kids, either gum or candy. The children thought he was wonderful, but not just for the treats. He had a special password he'd say when he'd get out of the car. The kids would always respond with "Fum," and give him a high five. Wonderful memories of very special times!

Tom bought two aluminum lawn chairs to put in the side yard. That way, we could sit and keep an eye on the boys when they were outside. One hot evening, Pop came over and Tom set up the chairs. It was actually cooler outside; the apartment could get quite hot during the summer. Tom and Pop watched the boys play in the yard while I cleaned up from dinner.

Pop was a tease and tried to catch Tommy by his shorts. But his chair tipped sideways onto the cement walk, and he was hurt. We hurried the boys upstairs and Tom called Mike to help get Pop to the hospital. It turned out that Pop had broken his hip, and it was the start of his decline. He never went home again.

Pop went to live with the Bannans until Father Pete's dad became ill with cancer. Pop was requiring increasing care, so his children found a nursing home for him out in the country. We'd take the children to see him as often as possible. He had one good friend, Mr. Brown, at the home, and seemed to do fairly well until the last few months of his life.

MOVING TO OUR FIRST HOME

We had lots of fun with our two little boys. When Bob was one-and-a-half I found I was pregnant again. The apartment was great, but it would be too small for three children. We had been saving Tom's National Guard money, and we decided to go house hunting.

Three-and-a-half years after we were married, we bought our first house, a nice 3-bedroom rancher in New Windsor, just outside of Newburgh. The address was 4 Rocky Lane, and it was on a dead-end street, which meant very little traffic. It had been owned by a couple in their 80s, and it was getting to be too much for them, but it was in great shape. The house cost $15,000, which meant we would be buying it on a shoestring.

I talked to our realtor and explained how little money we had, so she agreed to cut her commission by $200. The day of the closing, we borrowed money from Tom's brother Mike and sister-in-law to have "just in case." It turned out that we didn't need it at all. We moved in during July 1961. Our friends—the Conklins, Burgers, and Leghorns—helped us move, and we needed all of them. It was quite a job! Tom swore we would never move ourselves again.

One of the things I liked about our location was that we were in St. Joseph's parish, the very same parish where I went to church when my mother and I visited the farm, and then when I lived there.

The first weekend we were in the house, our next-door neighbors—Stanley and Clara Zgrodeck—had a big party to celebrate their son's second birthday. They had been married 13 years before their son was born, so every one of his birthdays was treated as a big event. Stanley, who was Polish, played mostly Polish music, and he did it, remarkably, by ear. He was very good on the accordion, harmonica, and spoons. They had a keg and all kinds of food that day. We didn't know them yet, but we sat in our back yard, and enjoyed the music and the celebration. Later, we told the Zgrodecks how much we enjoyed their party. They said, "You should have come over."

A few weeks after we moved in, our septic system backed up. Actually, our leach fields were broken and off-kilter. Tom talked to his friend Ira Conklin, who had backhoe equipment as part of his construction business. He told Tom to buy orangeburg pipe, and then he came over, dug up the old pipe, and with Tom's help, replaced it with the new. Some of our leach fields ran onto the Zgrodecks' property. When Stanley came home from work, Tom ran over to apologize and promise that he would fix his lawn. Stanley smiled and said, "Don't worry about it. Come over and have a beer. You need it after the day you've had." Thank God for Stanley's understanding and Ira's generosity. We had just moved into the house and had very little money.

Tom's brother, John, had just purchased a new lawn mower because the old one had a broken wheel. He offered it to Tom thinking that the wheel could be welded. We were glad to get it, but found that the mower was made of pot metal and couldn't be welded. Tom still managed to mow our lawn with it for years. He'd simply hold it a certain way and it worked well enough. It served a purpose, but Tom was happy when he could afford to replace it.

GROWING PAINS FOR TOMMY

One of our first purchases after we moved in was a sandbox for the boys. I invited Stash, (the Zgrodecks' little boy) to play with our boys. He wasn't used to playing with other children, and the first thing he did was fill a metal pail with sand and hit Tommy over the head with it, making Tommy cry. I scolded Stash and told him to go home. Clara (his mother) came over and asked what was wrong. After I told her, she said Tommy should do the same thing to Stash. I said "No. Two wrongs don't make a right. When he doesn't behave I will send him home." I had no more problems with Stash after that.

About a month after we were in the house, Tom had to leave for his two-week stint with the National Guard. His cousin Angela, who had been such a help to me, had met and married Bob Healy, a very nice fellow from Connecticut. While I was happy for her, it meant I didn't have my usual helper when Tom was away. A few years later, my friend Cissie would come and spend time with me when Tom was at camp. But for now, I was alone and had to work things out myself.

Tom had just left for Camp Drum, in Northwestern New York, when Tommy fell off the front step and refused to put weight on one of his legs. Our regular pediatrician was on vacation, so I took Tommy to the doctor who was taking her calls. He told me to go to Children's Hospital in New York City, which really upset me. There I was, seven months pregnant, alone with an injured child and his 21-month-old brother. Tom called to see how everything was going and I related my tale of woe. Tom rushed home from Camp Drum only to find that Tommy had no problem with his leg anymore.

FIRE!

The first Labor Day weekend in our little home proved to be very exciting. Early Sunday afternoon, Pam and Ira Conklin, friends who had helped us move in, stopped to visit. Shortly after their arrival, a thunder and lightning storm rocked the area. Tom was sitting on our hassock fan when the plug actually flew out of the socket. We heard an odd noise in the basement, and when we opened the door to see what it was, flames were shooting out of the fuse box. Tom called Central Hudson Electric Co. to shut off the electric, and everything was all right for awhile. The Conklins left and Pete Bannan stopped in.

A truck from Central Hudson Electric Company soon arrived and a repairman climbed the utility pole that held the transformer. When he turned the switch on, there was a vibration under the floor—similar to a vacuum cleaner—and the flames once again started to flare out of the fuse box. Pete and I grabbed the boys, who had been napping, and ran outside with them.

Tom soon followed and told the electric company worker (who he knew) to cut the power to our house. Given the smoke, the smell, and the sense of danger, we called Mom & Dad and asked if we could spend the night at their house. Just as we were preparing to leave, the telephone rang. It was Uncle Mike calling to tell us that Aunt Alice had died.

Even though Aunt Alice was only 61, I felt it was a blessing for her and the Donovan family that she finally let go after the severe stroke she had suffered 10 years ago. I'll always remember going with Aunt Helena to see her shortly after she was placed in the nursing home. She told Aunt Helena not to bring me again; Aunt Alice thought I had seen too much sadness in my young life. The wake and funeral were to be held in Newburgh, and she was to be buried with the Donovans.

The day after the electrical fire—Labor Day—we returned home. An electrician came and installed a bigger and better fuse box, and also put up a lightning rod. Fortunately, the insurance paid for our electrical problems and, with a little painting and cleaning, we were as good as new.

THE FAMILY GETS LARGER

On October 18, 1961, our first little girl was born. We named her Kathleen Mary after both of her grandmothers. She was a big baby—8 pounds, 15 ounces—and a little angel.

We had wonderful neighbors on both sides of our home. The Cimorellis (the man who built our house) lived on one side and the Zgrodeks lived on the other. Joe Cimorelli was in the construction business and came across an old metal swing set on the grounds of one of the properties he was building. It was a little rusty, but he asked us if we'd like to have it for our children. We were delighted! Joe delivered it and we fixed it up. The children used it for three or four years until it fell apart. But by then we were able to afford a replacement.

Our boys knew the boundaries of our property and were told to stay in the back yard. Even so, I think I spent half my time checking to see where they were. When Kathy was about a month old, I took her to her room to change her., and when I returned, the boys were gone. Frantically, I called Marie Cimorelli to see if they were with her because she often invited them to her back step for treats.

Marie said, "Yes they're in my kitchen having cookies and milk." Just before my call, she had said to the boys, "I should call your Mommy and tell her where you are." Tommy said, "Don't bother, she won't care." I said, "I sure do. I was scared when I didn't see them in the backyard." The children were great and, after that incident, were very good about staying in their own yard.

I always said I could have done my housework in a fraction of the time if I wasn't looking out the window every two minutes to check on them, but it was worth it and I knew it. They were wonderful playmates and were good about looking after each other.

We didn't know anything about an Italian tradition that all kinds of fish are cooked for the family to share on Christmas Eve. At least not until Marie Cimorelli rang the doorbell with a very large platter of fish for us. She did this every Christmas that we lived next to each other. And the fish was wonderful.

Joe and Marie were about 15 years older than Tom and I. They called us "the kids." Their son, Gerald, was about five years younger than Tom, but they served in the National Guard together. Gerald was married to a girl named Vickie, and they had a little girl, Debbie, who was a year older than Kathy.

111

Since Marie's granddaughter was too young to enjoy Santa, Marie asked if she could take Tommy and Bobby—who she loved—to see Santa at Schoonmaker's Department Store. I had an infant to take care of, and Tom used our car to get to work, so I thought it would be great for the boys. They had a terrific time and Marie bought them little things. She told me someone thought the boys were her children, and she took that to be quite a compliment.

When Marie and Joe would go on vacation they would ask me to feed their two collies, Lucky and Lassie, and let them out. Our children loved the dogs and it was no problem. All I had to do was walk across the side yard.

To repay us, the Cimorellis turned half of our basement into a playroom. Joe bought wood paneling to finish off one side from the furnace room and put up ceiling tiles. We thought it was a high price for them to pay just for dog sitting, but they were great to us. We painted the other three walls in a light yellow on top and beige on the bottom. Tom made a big toy box so all the toys would be downstairs. The children used this room a lot in bad weather. They also slept there on very hot nights, on two sofas that could be made into double beds.

You can't turn your head for a second

When Kathy was about nine months old, I was using a diluted bug killer in the backyard to get rid of Japanese beetles. Kathy was sitting in the playpen and the boys were playing in the sandbox. About noon I called to the boys that it was time for lunch and they needed to go to the bathroom and wash their hands.

I had the little vial of bug killer, no bigger than a bottle of vanilla in my hand. I didn't have any pockets, so after the boys went inside I set it on the milk box by the back door. I bent to pick up Kathy from the playpen, and as I turned around the door had closed. Tommy had reached out and taken the bottle. He took the top off the bottle to have a taste, and gave some to Bob, saying, "Daddy's beer."

I grabbed the bottle and threw it over the stone fence at the back of the property, that was a foolish thing to do because the doctor would want to know what they ingested. With Kathy in my arms, I ran with the boys to Marie's. She drove us to the hospital emergency room where our pediatrician was ready for us. She told me to stay in the waiting room with Kathy while she pumped the boys' stomachs. She said, "I guarantee they will never do anything like this again."

Tom came home for lunch, but was met by our neighbor, Clara Zgrodeck, who told him the boys had drank poison and were at the emergency room. Tom got in the car and just about flew to the hospital. When he arrived, the boys were sweating and teary, but past the ordeal of having their stomachs pumped.

FRIENDS AND RELATIVES VISIT

The first time my friend Cissie came to Rocky Lane, she and her daughter Maureen—who was about six months older than Tommy—had taken the train from New York City, and then a cab to our house. We hadn't known when she would arrive and Tom and I were running errands when she got there. Mom was at the house baby-sitting for Kathy.

When we pulled up, Cissie came out to greet us. I told her I was so sorry we weren't there for her arrival. She said, "Mrs. Gilligan and I were having the best time visiting and having a cup of tea." Mom agreed that she enjoyed Cissie, too, because Cissie was so easy to talk to.

Cissie lived in the Bay Ridge section of Brooklyn and always referred to our home in New Windsor as being "in the country." She spent time with me every year when Tom was away with the National Guard, outside of the year that her son John—who is about Kim's age—was born. Cissie's husband, Tom, worked for the railroad and she received free train passes. I enjoyed Cissie and her children.

One day, I answered the doorbell and found a clean-cut young man, probably in his late teens, standing there. He said his car had overheated and he needed water for his radiator. Not knowing anything about cars, I filled a quart pitcher with water and handed it to him. A few minutes later, he returned the pitcher and asked if he could use the bathroom. Being trusting and naïve, I said sure. He was in the bathroom so long I became nervous and picked up Kathy and took her and the two boys next door to Clara's.

I asked Clara to come back to the house with me. I knocked on the bathroom door and said, "One of the children has to use the bathroom and my husband is on his way home for lunch. Please leave." He left, without so much as a thank you. Tom told me that a quart of water wouldn't have helped if a radiator was overheating. I don't know what the young man was up to, but it was obviously no good. I learned a valuable lesson: Don't be so trusting.

The following spring the doorbell rang and I answered it. There was a young man who I assumed was a salesperson. I was busy and told him I didn't need anything, and closed the door. The doorbell rang again. This time the fellow said "Pop is in the car. I'm your cousin, Mark Kennedy." I didn't really know Mark, but I was aware of him. I really felt bad being so abrupt. It was near noon, so I invited them to stay and have lunch. We enjoyed a nice visit, and had a few laughs at my expense.

TOM GETS A NEW JOB AND A NEW BODY

In the fall of '62 many changes started to occur in our lives. Tom was told that Eastern Acceptance Corporation was going to move to Virginia. He was offered a job at the new office, but we would have to pay our own moving expenses. We couldn't afford that kind of expense, plus we were expecting again, this time in June.

Fortunately, Eastern offered to pay Tom's salary until he found work. Tom filled out application after application with no results. Those first few weeks were depressing. But then he got four job offers, all at practically the same time. One was from a bank, one from an insurance company, one from a cigar manufacturer, and one from Dupont, which was Tom's #1 choice. When he went to his interview at Dupont, Tom was told he'd be hired if he could pass the physical.

Dr. Vincent, the Dupont doctor, told Tom he had to loose 40 of his 240 pounds and get his blood pressure down before he could be hired. All those after-dinner snacks, ice creams, and Pepsi Colas we both ate and drank regularly had taken their toll on Tom. With my metabolism in those days, I didn't gain an ounce.

We gave up the evening snacks and Tom started eating half a sandwich for lunch. In a short time he went back to Dr. Vincent for a weigh-in and blood pressure check, and he was hired. To this day, Tom watches his weight and is glad that Dupont insisted on his taking control of his weight. He feels it keeps most health problems at bay.

ADDING TO THE HOUSE AND FAMILY

Soon after we moved into our house, our friend Jack Burger came over and helped Tom build an outdoor picnic table with attached benches. And our friends, the Crowleys, had a dressed-up picnic table in their kitchen with unattached benches. Tom decided he could make one like that for our dining area.

At the time, we had a wrought iron dinette with a pink Formica top and cushions. It wasn't big enough for the six of us, let alone when company came by. We thought about buying a larger one, but it was too expensive.

Tom made a beautiful table and unattached benches and stained them with an Early American finish. He bought two captain's chairs and stained them, as well. The set not only looked great, it served our family for nearly 40 years. Now our daughter Kathy is enjoying her father's handiwork.

We had our second little girl, Kimmy, on June 1, 1963. At the time, the boys were 3-1/2 and 4-1/2 years old, and entertained each other constantly. Kathy was 1-1/2, very placid and already potty-trained. It's a good thing those three were low maintenance because Kimmy was not the easiest baby to take care of. But we enjoyed her, nonetheless.

Shortly after she was born, we bought our first station wagon. At first, Tom thought it would be great for us to have two cars, so we kept my '56 black and white Chevrolet. But having four very young children with nap schedules and requiring constant care didn't give me much time to drive around. So we decided to sell the Chevy and use the money to build a porch on the side of the house.

Tom dug the footings for the porch by hand, and got some of the fellows he knew from the National Guard to pour the slab. Actually, Tom had dug so deep they filled most of it with rock. When Marie Cimorelli discovered that we were building a porch, she sent her husband Joe over. He said he and his son, Gerald, would help.

This was Tom's first real carpentry experience. To this day, Tom will say he learned so much from Joe, including how to straighten a warped 2 by 4 (one of the tricks of the trade). The porch was built quickly and it gave us a lot more enjoyment than a second car at that time of our lives. We screened the porch and, every winter, we'd cover it with plastic held in place by wooden strips. This ensured that it wouldn't fill with snow. We used the porch as an entranceway where the kids could take off their wet boots.

It was quite a job to winterize it every year, so Tom decided to install jalousie windows and storm doors. As usual, he did a great job. Tom and I also put a ceiling on the porch. It was about 12' high and made out of plywood. We still laugh about our joint construction project: We used two ladders, lifted the plywood together, and held it in place as Tom nailed it. While Tom was nailing, he needed both hands so I'd have to bear the bulk of the weight. Sometimes it got so heavy for me, I would rest the plywood on my head, urgently telling Tom to "Hurry up!"

LIFE WITH
THE CHILDREN

I really followed a strict schedule with the children. They woke up, made their beds, ate meals, had snacks, and went to bed at a set time. I believe this gave them security and gave me the ability to keep up with my household chores without any problem. I like to stay organized. Not falling too far behind on my schedule really gave us the opportunity to enjoy our children more.

Sometimes one of the children will reminisce about the "parties" they had before bed. I would fill a small shaker three-quarters full of milk, put a scoop of ice cream in it, put on the top and shake it. Each of the kids was given a three ounce plastic cup filled with the shake and they thought they were in heaven.

In the winter, we'd ride sleighs, build ice forts, and go ice-skating. Tom would also play catch and basketball with the boys. When the first four were old enough, he'd take them, two at a time, to Cornwall to teach them golf. When they were small, I'd play "Big Bad Wolf" and "Operation" with them after my chores were completed. If anyone ever saw me they'd have thought I was crazy. If I had a college education I would have liked to teach kindergarten, first, or second grade. I love little children, they are so much fun.

When our neighbor's boy, Stash, started first grade, his mother went to work at the pocketbook factory where her husband worked. She asked me if I would see Stash off to school in the morning and take care of him after school, until she came home from work. I told her it would not be a problem since Tommy and Bob would be leaving and returning at the same time. She insisted on paying me and we agreed on two dollars a week. We probably broke even because on holidays from school Stash liked to eat the same lunches as our kids. But he was never a problem.

When Kim was about a year old, Helen Travers invited the children, Tom, and me to her Brooklyn home for lunch. She wasn't used to having little children around, but she worked very hard at pleasing them. She even bought toys for each one.

During the visit, Helen said, "You will never guess who came to see me about a month ago." I couldn't imagine. She told me there had been a knock on her front door and a nice looking, well-dressed man stood there. She didn't recognize him until he introduced himself as Brother Rooney. He told her he had lived on the streets for almost 15 years, then woke up one morning and wondered what he was doing with his life.

He sought help, gave up drinking, straightened out, and had been working as a jewelry salesman for the last few years. She said she couldn't believe how well he looked and acted like his old self. He came by because he knew that she cared, and he wanted her to know that things had turned out well. I was delighted because he was such a good person. It was nothing short of a miracle.

With four small children, there was a lot of wear and tear on our upholstered furniture and car seats. I decided to make slipcovers, and measured and bought fabric. I started with the car seats because they were easy. Then I graduated to our upholstered chairs and couch. They were much more difficult because I was working with bulk.

There was a door-to-door salesman who stopped at the house once a month. He sold sheets, pillowcases, blankets, and, believe it or not, slip covers. I was struggling to get my slipcovers done one afternoon when he appeared at the door. He asked what I was doing and when I told him he got a big smile on his face and said, "This is great. You can alter the slip covers I sell." I said "Oh no! I can't wait to get done. I don't want to work on another slipcover until these are worn out."

I was very pleased with myself when they were finished. I made a few pairs of slipcovers for the cars and furniture. They saved wear and tear on the furniture and I washed them twice a year. They made everything feel nice and clean.

SOCIALIZING WITH NEW FRIENDS

Most of our social life took place at church meetings, fairs and dances. In the fall of '64 we went to a Halloween costume dance with our usual friends. We met a new couple, Anne and Bill Galvin, who had just moved into a development across the highway from our street. We had a great time and found the Galvins to be a lot of fun.

One Saturday we were visiting the Velices, fellow church members and the Galvins' next-door neighbors. Anne peeked her head out of a side window and said, "I have lots of spaghetti and meatballs." Come over to dinner." We all went and had a great time.

The holidays came and went and Tom's 30th Birthday was approaching—the big 3-0. I bought a steak (a rare occasion) and invited Mom & Dad for dinner that Sunday. Unfortunately, we had a blizzard and Mom and Dad bowed out. I suggested to Tom that since we had a steak and lots of other food, and that since the Galvins lived only a few blocks away, perhaps they'd join us. He said to call, but that anyone in his or her right mind wouldn't come out on a day like this.

I called and they said they'd be right over! Bill and Anne parked at the top of the street and walked down to our house with their 5-month-old daughter, Annie, bundled in a blanket. Then Bill trudged back to his car, drove to Midway Market, and bought beer. We had a wonderful afternoon and evening.

The next morning, Marie Cimorelli said, "Tom has a wonderful brother to come out in weather like yesterday's." I laughed and said they were our friends. And they still are.

Neither we nor the Galvins had much money, so for a little relaxation and fun we'd have a few beers and dinner at each other's house on Saturday or Sunday each week. Sometimes we would go to Bear Mountain or one of the nearby lakes for an afternoon. We became close friends without spending much money. As Tom said, "We have four star memories and a five star friendship."

Whenever we decided to go someplace, the four adults and eight children would all load into our station wagon. You couldn't do that today because of the seat belt laws, but we had a great time together.

Tom and Bill also helped each other with household projects, like painting and wallpapering. One weekend, Bill came over to help Tom paint porch trim. I was in charge of cleaning the brushes, but I splashed turpentine into my eyes and couldn't see. Tom called the doctor who said, "Wash her eyes with lots of cold water."

Tom sat me down on a chair in the kitchen, and he and Bill took turns filling pots with water and throwing the water in my face. Anne came in while they were dousing me and asked what was going on. I was soaking wet and so was the floor. Why I let them do that I'll never know, but they claim they saved my sight.

Another time, Tom went to Bill's house to help him put up wallpaper. While Tom was standing at the top of the ladder holding the wallpaper in place, Bill received a business call. He left Tom standing on the ladder with his arms outstretched for so long that Tom started to feel weak. They both teased each other about that for quite a while.

A few years after we built the porch, the Zgrodecks decided to do the same. They enclosed their porch and put a Franklin stove in it. A few weeks later, on a hot Sunday August afternoon, Bill came over, and he and Tom decided to see Stanley's new porch. They walked over and talked Stanley into lighting the stove. When the little ones got up from their naps, Anne came over and we decided to go next door, too. Tom, Bill, and Stanley were sitting in a very hot enclosed porch, drinking beer, eating hot peppers, and sweating like crazy.

FUN WITH TOM AND BILL

We all did some church work. Bill, who worked for a truck leasing company, would use a company truck when the church needed something moved, and Tom would usually be his helper. One day they had to move a number of large folding tables and chairs from the church basement to the church school.

Tom and Bill were in the cab of the truck after it was loaded, and a fellow by the name of Jimmy Pullar was in the rear with the tables and chairs. They had closed the back door, but it didn't catch properly. When Bill drove the truck up a very steep hill, the back door opened with tables, chairs and Jimmy sprawling on the road behind. Even though he wasn't hurt, Jimmy didn't think it was funny, although Tom and Bill couldn't stop laughing.

Another time, Tom and Bill went to pick up some pews for the Church. Bill had a cigar in his mouth when he missed the highway exit. He started to make an illegal u-turn, but a policeman waved him over. Bill forgot that his window was up as the policeman walked over. Bill turned to talk to the officer and his cigar hit the window, sending sparks flying in all directions. The policeman had a hearty laugh at Bill's misfortune and actually stopped traffic to let them turn around. These are only a few of the many great Galvin/Gilligan stories. We have had a wonderful time together.

TOMMY GOES TO THE HOSPITAL

When Tommy was about seven years old, he seemed to be having intestinal difficulties every two weeks. I took him to the pediatrician, who diagnosed a virus. I said I didn't think so, because we had four children in the house and none of the others was getting sick. The pediatrician asked if I knew a surgeon. I told her that Tom's Aunt Gin worked for Dr. Kearney. She suggested that I have him look at Tommy, and I agreed. But the surgeon said the same as the pediatrician. However, Tommy was a sick little boy and putting him in the hospital was recommended as an option.

Tom and I decided that was the best thing to do. The hospital called early the next morning and told us Tommy's blood count was way off and that he would require emergency exploratory surgery. We asked Mom to take care of the other children and rushed to the hospital.

During the operation, the doctors found he had something called Meckel's diverticulum, which is an inflammation of a pouch at the end of the small intestine that mimics appendicitis. It's usually no more than 2" long, but when it was removed it was the size of an orange. The doctors took it out along with his appendix and some intestinal tissue. Tommy was in the hospital for over a week and then came home to recuperate.

ANOTHER BABY, ANOTHER HOME ADDITION

When Annie Galvin was about two years old, Anne discovered she was pregnant again. When the baby was due, the Galvins dropped Annie off at our house and went to the hospital. Kim was thrilled because her number one friend was going to stay with us. By the time Billy Galvin was born on January 13, we knew we were going to have child number five.

With yet another baby, we needed more bedroom space and another bath. Joe Cimorelli had always been good to us, so we asked him for a price to build an addition and turn the garage into a family room. The price was right and we gave Joe the go-ahead. It was finished in plenty of time and he did a great job.

We put a fireplace in our new family room, and it gave us six wonderful years of enjoyment. Our son Jeff was born on June 13, 1967, five months to the day after Billy Galvin. Jeff had actually been due at the end of April but, as you might tell from his birth weight of 9 pounds, 5 ounces, he was about 6 weeks overdue. He was so overdue that his skin was peeling. But he was a wonderful baby, very content, and he seldom cried.

We enjoyed having a new baby in the house and so did Jeff's siblings. We often laughed that he was the little king. No parents could have loved and enjoyed their children more than we did. I think I relived my own childhood through them.

THE KIDS AND I
GO INTO SCOUTING

In the fall of 1967, Tom went to a meeting at St. Joseph's School to discuss creation of a Cub Scout troop. Tom had been involved with scouting as a boy and thought that our boys would enjoy it. When he returned from the meeting, he told me how difficult it was to get leaders for the Cub Scouts. I asked if they finally got the people they needed, and he said they had. But because of the number of boys interested in scouting, they needed two troops and required a leader for each one.

Tom told me that Nancy LaStrange was one of the leaders and, since we had two boys going into the Cub Scouts, he had volunteered me for the other troop. I told him that was impossible since Jeff was only three months old. He said, "You'll work it out." And, of course, I did. We brought our small picnic table down to the furnace room where I had my meetings with the boys. Tom also brought down the playpen for Jeff, who was such a good baby he was never a problem. And during the meetings, the girls were happy to be in the playroom.

When we bought our second car, we took the Cubs to visit local historical sites such as General Knox's and George Washington's Headquarters. We also worked on projects such as making homemade kites and showing the Cub Scouts how to fly them. I enjoyed working with children so much that I became a Girl Scout leader when our girls were ready for Junior Scouts. I taught the girls how to cross-stitch and use a sewing machine, and how to camp. I was also a Cub Scout leader for Jeff and was involved in the committee for Boy Scouts in Anderson, SC. It was fun and I don't regret doing it.

When our children were young they knew that the word "bored" was not to be mentioned around their mother. All they had to say was, "I'm bored," and I'd give them a dust cloth to do the baseboards or some other chore. Needless to say, there was always something to be done in the house. Some of the children would volunteer their services to help me out now and again.

TOM GETS
PNEUMONIA

When we were young, it was "cool" to smoke. No one knew there were any health consequences. Tom never smoked at work, but when he was relaxing in the evenings or on weekends at home, he had cigarettes. I was a social smoker (Tom always said I bummed them) and enjoyed a cigarette with a cup of coffee or a drink.

In November of 1967, Tom got pneumonia, was put on medication, confined to bed, and told he couldn't smoke. Bill Galvin, who came to see Tom almost every evening after work, brought a small TV to our bedroom from the basement and hooked it up for Tom. During this recovery period we missed a big 40th Birthday bash for Tom's brother, John.

Our three oldest children were going to St. Joseph's School at the time. During morning prayers their classes would pray for Tom's recovery. Bob was eight and in third grade, when his teacher, a nun, asked how his father was doing. Bob said, "I think he's doing a lot better. Yesterday Mr. Galvin stopped to see him after work and they were drinking beer together." We told Bill and his reaction was a riot. He got a funny look on his face and said, "Oh no, we're planning on sending our children to St. Joseph's."

During Tom's recuperation, the doctor came to the house a few times. As Tom's health improved, he went to the doctor's office. During one appointment he asked the doctor when he could start smoking again. The doctor took a long drag on his cigarette and said, "I wouldn't if I were you."

Addiction is a terrible thing, even a smoking addiction. Tom was not a heavy smoker and never had another cigarette. Neither did I. Since then, our best man has died of cancer that ate away half his face, and another of Tom's old college friends died of emphysema. I guess we can say Tom's pneumonia was a blessing in disguise.

Taking care of
the Galvin children

In the fall of 1967, the Galvins were told there would be an addition to their family. And in July 1968, Patrick Ryan was born. He was a cute little blond baby, but he was born with a double hernia that required two surgeries. He also had problems with ear infections when he was little.

One time, Bill and Anne went on a business trip and Mrs. Gallagher, Anne's mom, was babysitting. During their absence I called to see how Mrs. Gallagher was doing. She told me Pat was quite sick with an earache. I told her I'd be happy to bring him to our house so she could enjoy Billy and Annie more.

I brought Pat to our house but, by the afternoon, he was running a high temperature. I put him down for a nap along with Jeff and called the doctor, who still made house calls. The doctor arrived in about an hour and I took him into the room where the boys were supposed to be sleeping. Actually, Patrick wasn't asleep and when he saw the doctor and his black medical bag, he pointed at Jeff and said, "He's the one who's sick." Both the doctor and I laughed. It was so obvious which child was ill but Patrick wanted to avoid the shot. The Galvin children all had their parents' wit. They were a pleasure to be around. All of the Galvins were like an extension of our family.

KIM STARTS SCHOOL AND AUNT FRIEDA CALLS WITH BAD NEWS

Kim started kindergarten in the fall of '68. Soon after, we bought a Volkswagen bug. Having two cars and an agreeable child like Jeff made life a lot easier. I used to call him my little buddy. We shopped and ran many errands together. Jeff was such a cute, well-behaved little guy. And he was the youngest grandchild in the area. After his grandfather retired, both grandparents would join us for lunches.

On September 16, 1968, I received a call from Aunt Frieda. Uncle Mike had died of a sudden heart attack at the age of 77. He lived longer than anyone in his family ever had.

A few months earlier, his license had been suspended because he pulled out onto a main road and caused an accident. He was told he'd have to go to driving school and take a driving test to get his license back. It's so interesting how things happen: Lottie, one of the ladies from whom I had rented a room before I was married, owned a driving school and Uncle Mike hired her to give him lessons.

I didn't know my uncle had had an accident or went to Lottie's driving school until I spoke to Aunt Frieda. I think he was still driving for the Savings Bank at the time of the accident, so that meant the end of his job. It must have been very difficult for Uncle Mike to run errands, grocery shop, and get to church since he lived out in the country.

Lottie had driven Uncle Mike to Newburgh to take his test, which he passed. As Lottie walked to the car to get Uncle Mike, he slumped over the wheel and died. It was a terrible shock to my Aunt, who had been married to him for nearly 14 years.

Aunt Frieda was a great lady who had had many heartaches in her life, including the loss of her daughter Dotty. But she always remained positive. Whenever we came to Newburgh after our move south, we'd stop for a visit and take her out to lunch. She always had great stories to tell. She spoke beautiful English, but we got a kick out of her German accent. Her "w's" always sounded like "v's." Aunt Frieda lived into her middle 90s, passing on in 1995.

When Aunt Frieda sold the farmhouse, she gave me a candy dish and my grandmother's dishes. She also gave me my grandmother's bed, the one in which I slept while I lived with my uncles. It was a timely gift because we were getting ready to put Jeff in a bed. That bed remained Jeff's until he went to college. After Tom's mother died, Mike and Dianne gave us her bed, as well. We had it refinished and, believe it or not, it's a pretty close match to my grandmother's bed. We have them in the same room, and our grandchildren enjoy their comfort today.

These old family pieces are real treasures to us. Our children and grandchildren are real treasures, too. They surprised us with a beautiful Hoosier cabinet for our 40th anniversary. We put it in the kitchen of our home in Seneca. It looks just like my grandmother's Hoosier cabinet from the old farmhouse. Great memories!

SUMMER FUN

The Galvins decided to rent a summer cottage in Brant Lake, New York. The lovely cottages were modern, available in two and three bedroom models, and were situated on the beautiful shores of Brant Lake, not far from Lake George. The community had a private beach that was safe for children, as well as a playground. You could play shuffleboard or take out aluminum boats for fishing.

When Jeff was about two years old, we also started going there. The rent was inexpensive and the cottages were maintained very well. Our family had a wonderful time. I remember Tommy and Bob burying Jeff in the sand. All you could see of Jeff—who thought it was great—were his neck and head. The only minor drawback was that you had to cross a road to get to the lake. The road, however, was lightly traveled and we were always with the younger ones when they crossed.

In 1972, after we had been summering at Brant Lake for three or four years, we had a call from the owners of the cottages. They were selling them and wanted to give the Galvins and us the first chance to buy. We were selected for early notification because we always left the property in perfect shape, and the owners wanted to sell to people who would take that kind of loving care.

The cottages were available to us at the great price of $10,000 each, but we couldn't afford it. Even if we went in with the Galvins, neither family could handle the extra expense. Today, that property is probably worth twenty five times as much, but as the old saying goes, "You have to have money to make money." How true.

LIFE IN THE EARLY '70S

In 1970, Dupont went on strike and the labor union picketed outside of the gates. Management was put on shutdown, which meant the white collar personnel stayed inside the plant for two weeks and food was brought in from the outside. Twice, Tom drove our VW bug home to see us. And both times when he returned to the plant, strikers jumped on the car and tried to overturn it. Tom just kept moving forward.

Thank God, the union people didn't succeed in harming Tom or the car. When the strike ended, Tom had the beginnings of an ulcer. So we decided to use the extra money earned during the strike to take a much-needed vacation. We went to Jekyll Island, Georgia, with the children and had a wonderful time. Tom seemed better when we returned.

After we came home, we had a little extra money and decided to use it to buy a 15' X 27' above ground pool. This involved leveling and sifting the soil in the backyard, and we did all the work ourselves. It was a big job and the two older boys helped quite a bit. We got three years of enjoyment out of that purchase.

Tom had a very close friend from college, Bob Crowley, who had married a girl named Mary Lou. Tom had been in their wedding party and was Godfather for their daughter, Kim, the oldest of the six Crowley children (Kim, Tim, Kathy, K.C., Bobby, and Mary Beth). We've stayed close to them through the years.

Not long after we got our pool, we made plans to meet the Crowleys in a park that was halfway between us. We had decided beforehand to swap some of the children for a week. The Crowleys would take our two girls and we'd take their three boys. We thought it would be fun to drive all six boys to the Catskill Game Farm. On the way there, we had car trouble that slowed us up for about an hour. Luckily, we weren't too far from a garage owned by an honest mechanic.

Once we got to the game farm, Tom bought crackers for each of the boys to feed the animals. Tim Crowley kept offering one of his crackers to a llama, then pulling it back. Finally, after much teasing, Tim finally let the llama have it. And the animal returned the favor. He apparently had had enough of Tim and spit the cracker back at him. We all had a good laugh at Tim's expense.

Another day during our children-exchange program, the five oldest boys went swimming in our backyard pool. (Jeff was only three and was napping.) From the rear window of the house, I could see the boys throwing their bathing suits out of the pool. I waited a few minutes, then went out and collected the suits and took them into the house. In a short time there was lots of pleading coming from the pool for the return of the bathing suits. I let them worry for about five minutes. Then, much to their relief, I walked back out and threw the suits into the pool.

MOM AND DAD GILLIGAN

During the summer of '72, Tom's Dad was having health problems that were getting progressively worse. His legs itched so badly he would scratch them until they bled. The doctors said he had uremic poisoning. In early December, Dad was hospitalized and, on the evening of December 15—Tommy's 14th birthday—we received a call that Dad had passed away. It was really touching that he was taken on that day, because he always had a very special relationship with Tommy. Dad was a nice man, but I think it was difficult for him to show affection because of the way he was brought up.

Tom was the youngest of four boys. His brothers were all married to girls from Newburgh and lived in Newburgh. Shortly after we moved back to the area from Fort Benning, his brother, Bud, who worked for General Motors was transferred. He and his wife Gladys moved to Connecticut with their four boys. Their fifth son, Peter, was born there, and their sixth son, Christopher, was born after they moved to Nanuet, New York.

About ten years later, Mike and Dianne—along with their six children—were transferred to Massachusetts, where Mike worked for Prudential Insurance. That left only two brothers in Newburgh, John and Tom. John and his wife, Joan, had five children. After Dad died, Joan and I took turns taking Mom, who didn't drive a car, grocery shopping.

One day when I was taking Mom home, I stopped to get gas at Jimmy Pep's service station. I introduced Mom to Jimmy and Jimmy came around my side of the car. He asked, "Do you know what storm sewers are for?" I told him I didn't know what he was talking about, and he hit me with the punch line: "They're for mothers-in-law. You give them a little push and it's goodbye." We had a good laugh and, as I pulled away, Mom said, "There's a man with a good sense of humor."

Jimmy Pep was great to us. Once when the car badly needed servicing, Tom took it to him and the total cost was $300, a lot of money back then. Tom looked at the bill and wondered how we were going to pay it. Jimmy told him there was no rush, and we gradually paid it off. Jimmy always kept our cars running smoothly, even when they were up in age.

THE GILLIGANS
MOVE TO CONNECTICUT

In the spring of '73, Tom was given a nice promotion that necessitated a move to Connecticut. At first he commuted so the children could finish their school year.

Tom was now working in Westport, a wealthy suburb in Fairfield County. The prices of real estate there were unaffordable, four or five times what our house in New Windsor was worth, and much smaller. We finally found a fixer-upper in Orange, Connecticut, east of Westport, that had been owned by a physician, Dr. Bernie Seigel, who apparently never disciplined his five children. The house was a wreck.

I was suffering from sticker shock. The price of our new house was $55,000 compared to the $35,000 we could get for our New York house (which in today's market, could probably fetch about $200,000). In 1973, when you could live well on $6,000 a year, that was a big difference. I could feed our family of seven for $25 a week. Of course I budgeted, using a little red clicker with which I would add my purchases. If I went over what I wanted to spend, I'd put back items that weren't essential.

The evening we left our house on Rocky Lane forever, Tommy graduated from South Junior High. It was a very emotional day for me because I loved the house in which we had raised our children, and I was leaving my friends. In retrospect, some of that emotion was rather foolish since we were only moving an hour-and-a-half away.

The new house was a bi-level. You walked onto a landing that had one set of steps leading up to the main floor and another going down to the lower floor. The upper level included a large, beautiful kitchen with cherry cabinets, a big living room and dining room, and 3 bedrooms with 2 bathrooms. The lower level had an enclosed playroom (very dark), along with a front room we didn't need. We took down the wall between the two rooms, added a support beam, and turned the space into a larger, more airy playroom.

There was also a large bedroom and bath downstairs that became Tommy and Bob's (Kathy, Kim and Jeff slept upstairs with Tom and me), as well as a laundry room, sewing room, and two-car garage. We had a beautiful backyard with an in-ground pool surrounded by inlaid brick. (One weekend when the Galvins came to visit, Bill laid on the bricks and got so burned you could see the outline of the bricks on his back.) The pool was large enough to accommodate a diving board. And the yard also had a built-in wooden play area with swings, a little lookout fort, and a glider. The children called it the "what-not."

I wondered how we could afford this promotion, even though I was always pretty good with a budget, Tom worked hard, and we managed. Everybody pitched in and fixed up the house. The Conklins and their two boys even came over to help a few times. We painted and papered the inside, replaced a few doors, and our older boys painted the outside.

Before we left Newburgh we found Kathy had won a trip to Europe with three other 6th graders from that area. This was the result of an essay she had written early in the year. Two local teachers were needed as chaperones. Danny Bannan, Tom's cousin, and his wife Debbie, who were newly married at the time volunteered, with a little persuasion from us. During the trip they visited London, Paris and Madrid. Thanks to Debbie and Danny's guidance and protection Kathy and the other children all have wonderful memories they can carry thru life.

Bob had been taking drum lessons in New York and we found another good drum teacher in Hamden, Connecticut, about a 45-minute drive from our new home. Early one Saturday morning I drove Bob for lessons but, after we were there just a short time, it started to snow. I thought the roads would be fine by the time the lesson was over, but that sure wasn't the case.

To get home, I had to get back on the highway and go through a toll booth. I was going slowly and cautiously, but as I neared the toll booths I noticed that many people who stopped to pay couldn't get traction. Men had to push their cars through the booths, but I paid my toll and had no problem. I was driving the Volkswagen bug that had its motor in the back, giving the car traction. The roads were extremely slippery and I prayed all the way home. Tom was so relieved when we arrived.

Another thing that was new to us in Connecticut were the ice storms. One morning we awakened to find snow on the ground and glitter all over the trees. But there was no electricity. It was beautiful but treacherous, and there was no electricity in the entire area. The playroom had a fireplace, and that's where we all stayed and slept. I even cooked in the fireplace since we had an all-electric kitchen that wasn't functioning.

On the fourth morning of the power outage, I felt sorry for the children and decided to take them to Howard Johnson's for breakfast after Tom left for work. I thought it would be good for them to get a nice meal and enjoy the warmth. As we sat at the counter eating, I watched a roach go up and down the straws in front of me. I didn't say anything to the children. I wanted them to enjoy breakfast.

Just as Tom was ready to drain the pipes in the house and find a motel in which we could live, the electricity came back on.

BAD NEWS,
GOOD NEWS, BAD NEWS

We were in our house for only a few months when we received a call from Tom's brother, John. Mom, a 74-year old woman, had been mugged in broad daylight on Broadway in Newburgh. She was coming out of the bank after cashing a check for two dollars, when a 15 year-old boy knocked her down and took her pocketbook. She was hospitalized with a wound to her upper forehead and shoulder.

Tom drove the 1-1/2 hours to see her and, later, so did I. Poor Mom looked bad, her face so swollen she was hard to recognize. The police caught the boy who did it, but we don't believe anything was done to him. Newburgh had been the All-American City in '52, but was starting a downhill spiral. John and Joan looked after Mom at their home when she first came out of the hospital. A few weeks later Mom came to stay with us for a couple of weeks.

Early next spring, as I was painting the last door inside the house, Tom came home from work with news: We were being transferred back to Newburgh. He had been promoted and would be returning to Newburgh as Plant Manager. I was shocked but happy for him. He had worked hard, and this was a great opportunity. And we were going back to our hometown, which was also great!

In the meanwhile, we received a call that Helen Travers—who had been such a wonderful support to me after Miss Annie Mason died—had passed away. She had been in a nursing home in New York City for the last few years. We left for Brooklyn to pay our respects at her wake. There were two funeral homes, Kennedy's and Gallagher's, that were side-by-side across from Holy Cross Church. My parents were buried by Gallagher's and the Mason sisters and Sis Pigott were buried by Kennedy's. Miss Travers wake was being held at Kennedy's.

We entered the reception area that was crowded with Helen's friends and relatives. Two men, a middle-aged man and an older man, were sitting outside of the doorway when the older man asked in a very loud voice, "I wonder what happened to the little girl who was involved with these people?" I knew he was referring to me, but I was too embarrassed to speak up in front of all the people. I was sorry afterward, because it probably would have pleased him to know I did well.

136

HOME TO NEWBURGH

We decided we weren't going to wait until the end of the school year to transfer the children. It was March, and the friends the kids had made in school would be great for summer activities. We got in touch with a Newburgh realtor and found a new home in Campbell Hall, a nice development in the Washingtonville area, about a half-hour from Newburgh.

The house was a two story colonial, situated on a large lot, and ready for immediate occupancy. Everything went well. We sold our Connecticut home quickly, and the kids adjusted to their new schools, soon becoming involved in extracurricular activities. We loved our new home, even though we only stayed in the area for four years.

Jeff was entering first grade and was assigned to Mary Musso's class. Mary was the sister of our sister-in-law, Gladys. Tommy and Bob graduated from Washingtonville High School. After graduation, Tommy went to Marist College for a while, then transferred to Orange County Community College and lived at home.

One evening after dinner I left to run errands and, when I returned, found Tommy doubled over with severe stomach pains. The doctor told us to go to the hospital where we discovered that scar tissue from Tommy's old surgery—back when he was 7 years old—was obstructing his intestines.

Tommy was so sick after his operation. He was in intensive care for about a week, followed by another week of regular hospital care. When he finally left, the doctor insisted that Tommy get lots of rest, and he gave us a list of things he shouldn't do.

Bike riding was one of the prohibited activities, but every time I turned around he and the bike were gone. Dianne called to see how he was doing and I told her he looked terrible, he was too thin, and he wouldn't follow doctor's orders. Dianne said "Send him here. He'll listen to us." A few days later, I called Mike & Dianne at their Cape Cod home to see how Tommy was. They said he wouldn't listen to them, either. In fact, he had borrowed a bike from their barn and gone deep-sea fishing. He soon returned home.

The year after Bob graduated from High School was Kathy's junior year. And that's when we found that Tom would be transferred back to the home office in Westport, Connecticut. Bob had already decided to go to Bucknell University thinking he'd be relatively close to home.

After completing his first year of college, Tommy told us he wanted to transfer to the University of South Carolina. We figured he had two reasons for the request: One, he had buddies from Marist College who transferred there, and two, he wanted to be further away from Mom & Dad. He had been through so much with his health issues, we told him he could go with our blessings.

BACK TO
CONNECTICUT AGAIN

We let the other children finish the school year while we searched for a house in Connecticut. Once again, we discovered a nice one in Orange, the only affordable place we could find. It was a very hard move for Kathy, who was going into her senior year in high school.

This time, we bought a Cape Cod. The kitchen was too small for us, but there was a bedroom behind the kitchen we didn't need. So we had the wall taken down between the rooms, put up a support beam, and had a carpenter build a few cabinets to match the existing ones. I stained the cabinets and we polyurethaned them. Tom took out the old kitchen floor and had a new one installed. When the kitchen was finished, it looked great and gave us a large eat-in area.

There was a knotty pine den and bath on one side of the kitchen on the main floor. This would eventually become Mom Gilligan's bedroom and bath. The master bedroom and bath, dining room and living room were also on this floor. There were stairs in the front foyer that led to two bedrooms and a bath on the second floor. The girls had one bedroom and Jeff had the other.

There was a walkout basement below, and another bedroom and bath that became the older boys' room. We fully intended to get the basement playroom up-to-date, but we just never found the time. The basement also contained a large laundry room. There was an in-ground pool in the backyard that needed work. But we didn't stay long enough to get to it.

We were barely past the move-in period when we learned that Tom's brother John was moving to Indiana. That would leave none of Mom's sons near her, so we drove to Newburgh to take Mom to lunch and try to talk her into moving in with one of the families. This was a difficult decision for Mom because she had lived her entire life in Newburgh. Mom finally agreed to come live with us since we were the closest to the Newburgh area.

Mom had the only color television in the house. We only had one other television at the time, a black and white set that sat in the living room. One night after dinner, Mom had gone to her room to watch TV. She was sitting in her chair, and the girls and Jeff came in and sat on the floor. I sat on her bed.

Tom thought he'd be funny and sprinted across the kitchen into her room, jumping onto her bed. It was Mom's old bed from Newburgh and, as Tom landed on the bed,

139

both sideboards broke and the box spring and mattress crashed to the floor. Mom thought it was hilarious. We were all hysterical laughing. We propped up the bed on both sides with books. The next morning, I went to a number of furniture stores until I found a set of replacement sideboards.

One morning I went outside in my slippers to pick up the newspaper. I didn't realize there was ice on the driveway and, the next thing I knew, I flew up in the air and landed on my tailbone. I walked around very gingerly for weeks. When I'd take Mom to the hairdresser or grocery shopping, she looked like the 40-year old and I looked like the 79-year old. It was really tough getting in and out of the car.

Mom seemed to adjust to the move rather well, as did Kim and Jeff. Tommy and Bob were away at college, so they weren't affected much. But Kathy was unhappy, which we understood. She was in her senior year of high school, but there wasn't much we could do. The parents of some of her school friends offered to keep her for the year but, at that point in our lives, we wanted her with us. She was only 16, our responsibility, and we loved her.

Next stop,
South Carolina

In the spring, we realized we were in for another transfer, this time to a new plant in South Carolina. That meant Mom would have to make another decision. She decided that South Carolina was too far and opted to go to Cape Cod to live with Mike and Dianne after Kathy graduated from high school.

We thought Tom's new position would be temporary and would last only until the plant in Anderson got on its feet. So we kept our home in Connecticut, and Stauffer Chemical rented a home for us in Anderson. Kim started her junior year in high school and Jeff started the seventh grade. We were there only a short time when Tom was named Plant Manager. We were told to sell our house in Connecticut and buy one in Anderson.

For whatever reason, it was taking a long time to sell the Connecticut house, and the company finally bought it from us. Anderson was "Old South" at the time. The important thing was where you lived, where you went to church, and what your husband did for a living. Our Southern brethren did not love the Yankees, and being Catholic made it worse. I really didn't like being there. I used to ask, "What difference does it make what your husband does as long as he earns an honest living? I wouldn't care if my husband was a garbage man." I think some of the folks in Anderson were still fighting the Civil War.

Shortly after we arrived in Anderson I met Joe and Susan Zingaro and their three children: Gene—who was a year younger than Jeff and in his Scout troop—Joseph, and Allison. Joe had previously worked in the Newburgh plant before transferring to Anderson. We lived only about half a mile from the Catholic Church. Release time on Tuesday afternoons for the Catholic children to attend CCD was from 4 p.m. until 5 p.m., so I suggested that Susan spend the hour with me since she'd be so close to my home.

We would share weekly experiences with each other over a glass of wine. Some of the wine had been a gift and it was really bad. One day, Susan was upset by a J. C. Penney salesperson who ignored her while servicing people who were behind her in line. It was as if she was invisible. I told her the mistake she made was opening her mouth to speak. As soon as the sales lady heard her northern accent it was all over. We had lots of laughs and became pretty close friends until Joe was transferred to Connecticut a few years later. It took time for Anderson to change and it took time for me to adjust to the area. But both have been accomplished.

We surely fixed Tommy when we followed him to South Carolina! We were only two hours from campus, which may have been good for him and us. While Tommy was going to college he worked at the Steak & Ale restaurant and one of his co-workers was Lettie Matthews, a nice girl from Columbia, South Carolina's capital. Tommy and Lettie went together and, after graduating from the University of South Carolina, they were married. They settled in the area and raised three children: Jayson, Meggan and Patrick.

Being that close gave us a chance to get to know the children, at least until Tommy began to be transferred from place to place. There was also a span of seven-and-a-half years between Tommy's children and the other grandchildren, which meant his children had our undivided attention. Tommy and his family have lived in Tennessee, Pennsylvania, Kansas and, now, California. Tommy earned his Masters Degree while working for Butler Building in Kansas. He's done very well for himself and we are proud of him.

Jayson graduated from high school in Kansas and went to college for a year before enlisting in the army. He was in the service a short time when he was deployed to Iraq. We're proud of Jayson's service in Iraq, but were happy when he returned to the States. After finishing his commitment with Uncle Sam, he returned to college in California. The other two children are also in college: Meggan's in her final year of college in Kansas (she also spent a few months in Spain as an exchange student); Patrick transferred to California for his senior year of high school and just finished his first year of college out there, too.

When we moved to South Carolina, Bob was attending college at Bucknell, in Lewisburg, PA. He couldn't get home for Thanksgivings because of the distance, but he always came home for Christmas and summer vacations. In the summers, Bob worked in Greenville, about 30 miles from the house. He had a little Vega Chevrolet without air conditioning, and by the time he got home from work he'd be soaked with sweat.

He graduated from Bucknell in 1981 and got a job in Brunswick, Georgia. He worked for a while, but decided that to go anywhere with his Mechanical Engineering degree, he needed a Masters degree, as well. He was accepted at the Wharton School of the University of Pennsylvania, earned his Master's, and took a job with Data General in New Hampshire.

PULLING A
SECOND STORY JOB

This is rather amusing: After Bob was in his New Hampshire apartment for a while, I went to visit him, planning on staying for about a week. Bob went to work early in the morning and I decided to go grocery shopping so I could have a nice dinner ready when he returned. As soon as I closed the door to his apartment, I realized I was locked out and wouldn't be able to get back in until he came home.

I went grocery shopping anyway, assuming I'd be able to figure out a way to get in. I came back with the groceries and left them outside Bob's second floor apartment door. I walked to the back of the house and noticed a fire escape outside of Bob's bathroom window. There was a small cellar window at ground level, and I stepped on the top of the window frame, which enabled me to reach the fire escape. I went up the fire escape and reached the bathroom window, but it was locked. I thought if I could get hold of a butter knife, I could slip it between the window sashes and open the lock.

I went down the fire escape, knocked on an apartment door, and explained my dilemma to the tenants. They gave me a knife, which I promised to return. Back up the fire escape I went and, just as I thought, I was able to unlock the window, climb in, and retrieve the waiting groceries. I used the regular steps to return the butter knife.

I fixed a nice dinner and told Bob the story when he returned from work. He couldn't believe I told his "rough-around-the-edges" neighbors how I was going to use the knife. He worried that they might try to get into his apartment the same way. Bob cut a broom handle the length of the upper sash and wedged it between the upper and lower sash for security.

While Bob was working for Data General, he met Ainslye Wallace, the woman who would become his wife. One evening he went to an aerobics class and Ainslye, a very cute girl from Wellesley, Massachusetts, was the instructor. After they were married, Bob took a position with General Electric. They've since been transferred from Massachusetts to Wisconsin to Atlanta, Georgia, where they currently live. They have two boys, Bobby and Christopher, who we enjoy very much. They live less than two hours away and, thankfully, we visit back and forth.

UPDATING THE FAMILY

Kathy spent a year at Dickinson College in Pennsylvania, but didn't go back. She came home to Anderson and accepted a secretarial job with Nordson, a local company. After a start-up period, Kathy was transferred to Atlanta and, while working there, met her husband-to-be, Fernando, who is originally from Peru. Kathy later went to work for Coca Cola, for whom she worked until their first child, Frankie (Francisco), was about 18 months old. Then she retired to become a stay-at-home mom. They still live in Atlanta, and Frankie has a brother, Matias, who is six years younger. We get a lot of enjoyment from Kathy and her family and we see them quite often.

Kim graduated from Hanna High in Anderson, in 1981, and then went to the University of Georgia where she graduated three years later. After graduation she went to Boston to work for Marshall's and lived with Bob while she worked there. We feel that this move helped them become closer.

After about five months, Kim returned to Anderson and took a job with General Mills, where she met her future husband, David. She later went to work for Nabisco, earned her Masters degree during that tenure, and stayed until her second child was born. Kim and David have three children, Dylan and his two sisters, Madison and Carson. They've lived in Texas and Pennsylvania and are presently in Minnesota. We know the children well and they are a pleasure. Kim manages to get home to see us a few times a year, and we travel to see them also.

Jeff graduated from Hanna High in 1985, and then went to Providence College in Rhode Island, where his dad had gone. Jeff graduated in 1989, and then settled in Columbia for a while. One of his friends introduced him to a sweet southern girl from Marion, South Carolina, named Tammy Dew. At the time, Tammy was earning her Masters and Doctorate degrees at the University of South Carolina (she had taken her undergraduate work at Clemson). While they were dating, she accepted an internship from the University of Nebraska.

Jeff had become involved in fundraising. He worked for Muscular Dystrophy and the Arthritis Association before accepting a position with a retirement community. He was transferred to Washington D.C. and Pennsylvania, but continued to see Tammy. On one weekend, Jeff traveled to Nebraska to ask Tammy to marry him. As a couple, they've lived in Pennsylvania and presently are residing in Virginia. Tammy is a psychology professor and Jeff is a manager in the Department of Development for James Madison University, where he's also working toward a Masters.

Jeff and Tammy have a girl and a boy. The girl, Addison Brandes (Addie or Addie B), is named after Tammy's and Jeff's grandfathers. The name Brandes—my maiden name that I was so worried about as a child—still lives on. The boy, John Riley (Jack), is named after Tom's father (Jeff's other grandfather), and Riley is just a good Irish name that seems so right. Jeff and Tammy live about seven hours from us and we get to visit back and forth and enjoy their family.

We manage to visit all of our children and grandchildren a few times a year and we enjoy their reciprocal visits. We sold our house in Anderson in 1997 and built a home in Seneca, South Carolina, where we can accommodate our five children and their families.

MOM GILLIGAN TAKES
A TURN FOR THE WORSE

Shortly after Mom moved to Cape Cod with Mike and Dianne, an obstruction in her intestines was discovered and the subsequent surgery showed it to be cancerous. It was about this time that Mom started to become confused. It was the onset of Alzheimer's disease. Tom and his brothers took six-month turns keeping Mom. Finally, Dianne and Mike said, "No more switching. She will stay here on the Cape with us."

In early August 1984, Mike and Dianne had a Prudential Convention to attend and I agreed to come to Cape Cod to take care of Mom. By then, Mom was bedridden, so I came a few days early to learn how best to care for her. She also had hospice care, which was a great help.

The hospice lady made an appearance one day around lunchtime, and I went to the kitchen to make a sandwich. Before I finished, the hospice lady called to me that "Mrs. Gilligan isn't acting right." I knew that was it. The date was August 9, 1984, and she was 85 when she died. Mom had been a wonderful mother-in-law and a great lady who never interfered in anyone's life.

More family tragedy

At the time of Mom's funeral, our sister-in-law Gladys (Bud's wife) was battling lung cancer. She put up a good fight, but succumbed a year-and-a-half later. Her family missed her so much, especially Bud and his youngest son, Christopher, who at the time of his mom's death, was still living at home.

Bud had worked for General Motors for many years. At his retirement party, he was given a bike, a great gift for someone living in Geneva, Illinois, where there are many wonderful bike paths. During one of his rides, he met a woman named Mary O'Brien and, after a period of dating, Bud and Mary married. Mary had had some terrible tragedies in her life, including the loss of her son in an automobile accident while he was at Clemson University. At the time of their marriage in 1988, Mary's daughter, Kelley, was finishing her second year at Clemson.

Since we lived so close to Clemson, we told Kelley to think of our home as her home away from home. She came over quite often, and spent the summer with us between her junior and senior years at college. We came to know Kelley very well and because we did, we saw Mary more than other members of the family. That made us closer and we are thankful for that.

MY BROTHER
PASSES AWAY

I didn't mention it earlier, but before the Zingaros moved to Connecticut, Susan had been working as a part-time service representative for Manpower Temporary Services. When they were about to leave, she asked me if I'd be interested in her job. I said yes and very much enjoyed working for Manpower. I made a few good friends in the office, and I think working there helped me to adjust to the area.

I was at the office on June 29, 1987, when Jeff called me. He said; "Mom, a Western Union Telegram was just delivered for you." I told him to open it and read it to me. He said, "It's about your brother. He's passed away." William died of emphysema at the age of 54. He really had a terrible life, the last 30 years of which had been spent in an institution. A very nice priest affiliated with Rockland State Hospital said a Mass for my brother in the facility's chapel. And thanks to a special waiver by the priests who ran the cemetery, William was buried at my parents' gravesite.

When we went to the hospital to get everything settled for the funeral and burial, I told someone on staff that I would like his clothing and belongings to be given to someone who could use them. I was given a large brown envelope with a few letters and personal things. Inside was a lovely letter from the priest who took care of Catholic patients at the institution, and also a Christmas card from my brother to a "Special Sister."

He had sent this card the Christmas before he died. It had been addressed to Campbell Hall, New York, but we had moved away eight years before he mailed it. Naturally, it had been returned to sender. There was a note in the card from William's caseworker that he would like to see me. It made me feel bad because I certainly would have tried to see him. But at least I knew he was thinking of me. Life isn't always the way we would like it.

We had visited my brother occasionally during his stay at Rockland State. During one visit, William's doctor asked how many children we had. I told him we had four, and he said it was our responsibility to raise our family, and it was his and his colleagues' responsibility to care for my brother. He promised to keep us updated on William's mental health. The doctor was right, because my brother threatened my family and upset us. The doctor said that people with mental problems always threaten the ones to whom they feel closest.

I will never understand why I was lucky enough to have a normal life and not he. Maybe because he was so much smarter than I was, or maybe because he suffered two fractured skulls when he was young. After our parents died he went from having a very structured, disciplined life to doing as he pleased. I can't blame Aunt Helena because she was a working woman with a very easygoing disposition, and she tried very hard.

TOM PUTS HIS MONEY AND HEALTH ON THE LINE

Stauffer Chemical Company was sold to Cheeseboro-Ponds in the mid-80s, then to Unilever, and then to ICI America. As part of the deal, ICI acquired the Anderson plant, but decided not to keep it. Tom and Cliff Gandis had worked together in management for years and contacted an investor from Atlanta, Georgia, to see if they could get backing to buy the plant. They also needed money from a bank, but most banks refused to see the plant, which manufactured decorative vinyl products, as a sound investment.

While these negotiations were going on, Tom went for a physical in the fall of 1987 and found he had prostate cancer. Surgery was scheduled for after the holidays at Emory Hospital in Atlanta. ICI's British management told Tom they would wait until he was back on his feet before going forward with the sale of the plant. In the spring of 1989 a bank in England accepted the deal, which was later taken over by The Bank of Boston.

Cliff and Bunny Gandis, along with Tom & I went to First Citizens Bank in Anderson. We signed over the ownership papers for our houses and most of the money for which we had worked our whole lives. By the time we left the bank we had about $1,500 to our name. The Atlanta investor gave us a great opportunity because of his expertise. The first few years were a little hard, but things straightened out and the plant started to make a nice profit. Tom sold his share of the company in the fall of 2001 and we are now able to do things we never dreamed possible.

Ten years after Tom's operation, the prostate cancer made another unwelcome appearance. The only thing left to do was radiation, and Tom undertook a nine-week regimen at Emory in August 1999. During the week, we stayed at a Residence Inn in Atlanta not far from the hospital, and came home to South Carolina on weekends.

The treatments were rough on Tom. We'd go to dinner every other night for a change of scenery. One night he became so sick after we placed our order, we paid the bill and left before we were served. In the middle of the process, Tom had to take a week off from the treatments because he was so worn down. After the radiation ended, he had to have injections of Lupron (a hormone) for about three years. This also took its toll, but now, a few years later, his PSA is zero and he's feeling like himself again.

SUMMER HOME

We decided to go to one of Tom's Providence College class reunions and stayed at an Inn in Maine owned by one of his classmates, Norm Dugas. Tom asked Norm where his help worked in the off-season, and he said they migrated to the Gasparilla Inn in Boca Grande, Florida. He also said how nice it was, and that he and his wife took a vacation there every year.

We decided to try it ourselves and we liked it. We stayed there for a few years, and then thought it would be fun to look around for a little house. We made an offer on one and I couldn't believe it when it was accepted. I must admit I was a little scared, but that's just me. We found a house at the right time because, about a year later, home prices went out of sight.

We now spend a little more then half the year in Boca Grande. All of our children and grandchildren enjoy it there, as well. Our cousin Pete spends a week with us every year before Lent starts, and we always look forward to his visits.

VISITING RELATIVES AND THE OLD NEIGHBORHOOD

My mother's youngest sister Regina—who passed away in 1977—had six children. About ten years ago I had the privilege of hearing from and meeting the three surviving children. Bill Anderson was the oldest of the six, and we met him and his wife, Natalie. They were a nice couple. Unfortunately, Bill had a bad case of emphysema and died approximately three months after we met. I was glad we had the opportunity to meet. We also met his brother, John, who was the next oldest. He lives in Vancouver, British Columbia. We've visited him a few times. He is a delightful man and we stay in touch.

The youngest, Ellen, is a Catholic Missionary Sister in Africa, and also a surgeon. We met her a few years ago, and she is quite a lady. She's told us about the poverty and AIDS epidemic there. She has put in a tremendous amount of time working in the hospital and helping the less fortunate. I stay in touch with Sister Ellen. She, Bill, and John have been very helpful in tracing the Donovan/Lynch clan with me.

During the holiday season in recent years, we've spent a few days visiting Father Pete at St. Catherine's Church in Pelham, NY. We also spend time in Manhattan and, during one of our trips; Tom asked if I'd like to go to Brooklyn and see my old Flatbush neighborhood, including Holy Cross Church and the cemetery where the Mason sisters are buried.

I wanted to go, but my friend Cissie told me the neighborhood had gotten very bad. She said it was like several sections of Harlem that were not safe. I was a little afraid, so we talked to Father Pete who said Harlem is safe as long as you are careful. He said it might be fun to go back, and so we went. It's always difficult to return to a place you loved and see such immense change. It was sad, but it was also fun.

Holy Cross Church had been renovated in the spring of 1944 when my mother died. There had been so much scaffolding in the church that her funeral mass was celebrated in Holy Cross Chapel, just down the street. These days, paint is peeling in the church, and it is obvious that it hasn't had any work done in many years, perhaps not since 1944. However, it was my Parish as a child and I have many fond memories.

Tom and I went to an 8 a.m. Saturday Mass and we were the only white people in the church. Even the priest was black. The people were very nice to us and asked us to bring up the gifts at communion.

After Mass, we had to ask for directions to the cemetery. So many years had passed, I wasn't sure how to get there. It was about a two-mile walk. The cemetery is very large and we couldn't find the main entrance. We asked a man for directions to the main gate and he was nice enough to guide us there. The cemetery office was very secure; we had to be buzzed in. The staff was amazed we had walked. They gave us a map to the grave, but we looked and looked for about 15-20 minutes without success.

Tom suggested we start at the opposite end and walk back, and told me to stay on the road since I was wearing sneakers and there was about five inches of snow on the ground. As we walked, I said a little prayer to find the Mason sisters' gravestone. I looked up and noticed a headstone with a granite cross on the top.

It had been 54 years since I had seen it, but I remembered it. I ran down the aisle of headstones and hollered to Tom that I had found the Mason sisters' site. Annie had always teased me. She said that when she died I should plant daisies on their grave and she would push them up from the bottom. I couldn't plant anything in the snow, but I said a little prayer for my Brooklyn angels and told them I would see them in the next life.

Not a day goes by that I don't pray for the Mason sisters. I thank God for giving me them and all the other wonderful people He sent to guide me in my young life. I still pray for guidance today.

The apartment on Bedford Avenue, where I spent the first six years of my life, is still there. But all the houses on Woods Place, and even the large auto repair garage, have been torn down. It looked as if construction had started on subsidized houses for the poor, but everything seemed to be at a standstill.

HEARTFELT THANKS FOR ALL OUR FRIENDS

There have been so many wonderful friendships over the years. Most have been mentioned in this book: Jack and Shirley Burger; Bob and Mary Lou Crowley; Ira and Pam Conklin; Bill and Anne Galvin; Tom (deceased) and Cissie Rohan; Harley (deceased) and Anita Rampe-Harley; Edward and Loretta Stenglein-Tryzinsky. And I will always have a special place in my heart for the parents of many of my friends, wonderful people who gave so much time and caring to make my young life smoother and happier.

Those close friends not detailed in my stories include Rene and Bob McCormick; Lynda and Larry Bowman; and, of course, Sam and Fran Leghorn with whom we were friends early in our married life but, between raising children and our many business moves, we weren't always able to maintain that close friendship. In later life, that friendship has been rekindled and we enjoy getting together a few times each year and staying in touch.

HEARTFELT THOUGHTS
FOR MY BELOVED FAMILY

When you have hardships in life, and everyone does, don't use them as an excuse to feel sorry for yourself. Pull yourself up by the bootstraps and go forward. Remember the good times and positive things you have learned from your experiences. I am so very proud of every one of you, I love you each in your own special way. You all have special, God-given talents and you are destined for great things in the future. Remember to always be honest, maintain your integrity, and fight for what you believe.

It is wonderful to have a family and see the closeness of brothers and sisters. So many times in my life I wished I was able to have a happy relationship with my brother. It is so nice to be able to reminisce and share a few laughs about the past. Try to keep your relationships with your brothers and sisters open always.

I often think that children today who might find themselves in the same situation I was would be put in foster care. There are many good foster parents, but some are only in it for the money. I have had a wonderful life and have had more people who cared about my welfare than most. I have no regrets.

The story of my life shows how God never closes one door without opening another. There are many good people in this world (as well as a few stinkers). One has to know how to choose.

Believe in God and yourself and you will get past many obstacles in life. Don't depend on others to assume your responsibilities. Work them out yourself, if at all possible. Last but not least, do not get into debt over your head because that can do nothing but cause problems. We know people who did, but we were always careful to avoid that trap.

If you do well in life and have the chance to help someone who's down on his or her luck, take the opportunity. It is good for the heart. Many times in my life, people considered my hardships and were there for me. I will never forget their kindness.

Everyone owes this world something: to live a good and meaningful life. Retain your honor and pursue every one of your dreams. They really are reachable. What a wonderful country we live in!

I don't know that I ever really thanked all the wonderful people who helped me through my life. I do thank God for giving them to me and I am sure he is rewarding each of them for their kindness toward me.

155

I want to thank you, Tom, for your patience while I spent so much time on the computer writing this story over the last few years. There always seemed to be another vignette to add or refine. You have been a spectacular father, spending lots of time with the children when they were young and just being there for them. You are also a good husband and a wonderful friend.

I want to close my life story with a verse that hangs on the wall inside our kitchen door. Dad and I both feel this from the bottom of our hearts.

To Our Children:

Look after each other
Encourage one another
Be kind—tender hearted
Keep your promises
Live in peace with one another
Remember life isn't always fair,
    But that's alright—
Take up for each other, being
    Loyal is a great treasure—
But remember, most of all, love
One another deeply from your
    Heart. ☺